Lab Manual for

Security+ Guide to Network Security Fundamentals

Second Edition

Paul Cretaro

THOMSO
COURSE TECHNOL

Australia • Canada • Mexico • Singapore • Spain • United Kingdom • United States

THOMSON
™
COURSE TECHNOLOGY

Lab Manual for Security+ Guide to Network Security Fundamentals, Second Edition
Is published by Course Technology

Managing Editor
William Pitkin III

Production Editor
Brooke Booth, Trillium
Project Management

Contributing Author
Kelly Cannon

Associate Product Manager
Sarah Santoro

Text Design
GEX Publishing Services

Product Manager
Amy M. Lyon

Technical Editor
Serge Palladino

Senior Marketing Manager
Karen Seitz

Editorial Assistant
Amanda Piantedosi

Compositor
GEX Publishing Services

Developmental Editor
Dan Seiter

Senior Manufacturing Coordin
Trevor Kallop

Quality Assurance Team Leade
Chris Scriver, Marianne Snow

Cover Design
Steve Deschene

ISBN-13: 978-0-619-21536-1
ISBN-10: 0-619-21536-4

BRIEF TABLE OF CONTENTS

Introduction — ix

CHAPTER ONE
Information Security Fundamentals — 1

CHAPTER TWO
Attackers and Their Attacks — 11

CHAPTER THREE
Security Basics — 25

CHAPTER FOUR
Security Baselines — 43

CHAPTER FIVE
Securing the Network Infrastructure — 61

CHAPTER SIX
Protecting Basic Communications — 83

CHAPTER SEVEN
Protecting Advanced Communications — 105

CHAPTER EIGHT
Scrambling through Cryptography — 143

CHAPTER NINE
Using and Managing Keys — 161

CHAPTER TEN
Operational Security — 179

CHAPTER ELEVEN
Policies and Procedures — 189

CHAPTER TWELVE
Security Management — 201

CHAPTER THIRTEEN
Advanced Security and Beyond — 211

TABLE OF CONTENTS

Introduction ix

CHAPTER ONE

INFORMATION SECURITY FUNDAMENTALS 1

    Lab 1.1 Risk Analysis—Definition of Assets 2
    Lab 1.2 Risk Analysis—Threat Assessment 4
    Lab 1.3 Risk Analysis—Risk Assessment 7
    Lab 1.4 Risk Analysis—Recommendations 9

CHAPTER TWO

ATTACKERS AND THEIR ATTACKS 11

    Lab 2.1 Using the At Command to Start System Processes 12
    Lab 2.2 Researching DoS and DDoS Attacks 15
    Lab 2.3 Researching the CPUHOG DoS Attack 17
    Lab 2.4 Researching the NetBus Trojan Horse 19
    Lab 2.5 Removing NetBus from an Infected System 21

CHAPTER THREE

SECURITY BASICS...25

    Lab 3.1 Using the Windows Server 2003 Local Password Policy Settings for Length 26
    Lab 3.2 Using the Windows Server 2003 Password Policy Settings for Complexity 29
    Lab 3.3 Preventing the Display of the Last Logon Name 32
    Lab 3.4 Setting an Account Lockout Policy 35
    Lab 3.5 Using the Run As Command to Bypass Security 39

CHAPTER FOUR

SECURITY BASELINES 43

    Lab 4.1 Defining Security Templates in Windows Server 2003 44
    Lab 4.2 Managing Windows Server 2003 Security Templates 48
    Lab 4.3 Protecting the System Accounts Database 51
    Lab 4.4 Configuring Services and Processes 53
    Lab 4.5 Configuring Network Settings 56

CHAPTER FIVE
SECURING THE NETWORK INFRASTRUCTURE **61**
Lab 5.1 Installing Snort on Windows-based Systems   62
Lab 5.2 Capturing Packets with Snort   64
Lab 5.3 Creating a Snort Rule Set   68
Lab 5.4 Using IDScenter as a Front End for Snort   72
Lab 5.5 Creating a Simple Honeypot   78

CHAPTER SIX
PROTECTING BASIC COMMUNICATIONS **83**
Lab 6.1 Configuring Internet Explorer Security   84
Lab 6.2 Configuring Internet Explorer Privacy   87
Lab 6.3 Configuring Internet Explorer Content Filtering   92
Lab 6.4 Configuring Internet Explorer Advanced Security Settings   97
Lab 6.5 Manually Blocking Web Sites and Pop-ups   100

CHAPTER SEVEN
PROTECTING ADVANCED COMMUNICATIONS **105**
Lab 7.1 Enabling Dial-in Access   106
Lab 7.2 Configuring a Windows Server 2003 VPN Server   108
Lab 7.3 Using PPTP to Connect to a VPN Server   111
Lab 7.4 Configuring a Remote Access Policy   113
Lab 7.5 Configuring a Wireless Access Point   118
Lab 7.6 Installing the Cisco Aironet 350 Wireless Access Point   125
Lab 7.7 Disabling Telnet Access to the Aironet WAP   129
Lab 7.8 Enabling the Aironet User Manager   132
Lab 7.9 Adding Administrative Users to the Aironet   136
Lab 7.10 Restoring the Aironet Factory Default Settings   138

CHAPTER EIGHT
SCRAMBLING THROUGH CRYPTOGRAPHY **143**
Lab 8.1 Using NTFS to Secure Local Resources   144
Lab 8.2 Ensuring Data Confidentiality   146
Lab 8.3 Ensuring Data Availability   150
Lab 8.4 Ensuring Data Integrity   154
Lab 8.5 Encrypting Data   156

CHAPTER NINE
USING AND MANAGING KEYS **161**
Lab 9.1 Installing a Certificate Server 162
Lab 9.2 Installing a Client Certificate 165
Lab 9.3 Administering a Certificate Server 170
Lab 9.4 Managing Personal Certificates 173
Lab 9.5 Managing Certificate Revocation 175

CHAPTER TEN
OPERATIONAL SECURITY **179**
Lab 10.1 Establishing Physical Barriers 180
Lab 10.2 Using Biometrics 182
Lab 10.3 Managing the Environment 184
Lab 10.4 Understanding Social Engineering 186

CHAPTER ELEVEN
POLICIES AND PROCEDURES...**189**
Lab 11.1 Creating Security Policies (Remote Access) 190
Lab 11.2 Creating Security Policies (Regulations) 193
Lab 11.3 Performing Risk Analysis 195

CHAPTER TWELVE
SECURITY MANAGEMENT **201**
Lab 12.1 Online Research—Awareness 202
Lab 12.2 Online Research—Education 203
Lab 12.3 Online Research—Standards and Guidelines 205
Lab 12.4 Online Research—Classification 207
Lab 12.5 Online Research—Retention and Storage 209

CHAPTER THIRTEEN
ADVANCED SECURITY AND BEYOND **211**
Lab 13.1 Transferring NTFS Encrypted Files 212
Lab 13.2 Installing ZDelete and Restorer2000 215
Lab 13.3 Using ZDelete Disk Wiper and Restorer2000 219
Lab 13.4 Installing Microsoft Network Monitor 222
Lab 13.5 Using Microsoft Network Monitor to Sniff an FTP Session 225

INTRODUCTION

Hands-on learning is the best way to master security skills necessary for both CompTIA's Security+ Exam and for a network security career. This book contains hands-on exercises that use fundamental networking security concepts as they are applied in the real world. In addition, each chapter offers review questions to reinforce your mastery of network security topics. The organization of this book follows that of Course Technology's *Security+ Guide to Network Security Fundamentals, Second Edition*, and using the two together will provide a substantial, effective learning experience. This book is suitable for use in a beginning or intermediate networking security course. As a prerequisite, students should have a fundamental understanding of general networking concepts, and at least one course in network operating systems. This book is best used when accompanied by the Course Technology textbook *Security+ Guide to Network Security Fundamentals, Second Edition*.

FEATURES

To ensure a successful experience for instructors and students alike, this book includes the following features:

- **Security+ Certification Objectives:** Each chapter lists the relevant objectives from the CompTIA Security+ Exam.

- **Lab Objectives:** Every lab has a brief description and list of learning objectives.

- **Materials Required:** Every lab includes information on network access privileges, hardware, software, and other materials you will need to complete the lab.

- **Completion Times:** Every lab has an estimated completion time, so that you can plan your activities more accurately.

- **Activity Sections:** Labs are presented in manageable sections. Where appropriate, additional activity background information is provided to illustrate the importance of a particular project.

- **Step-by-Step Instructions:** Logical and precise step-by-step instructions guide you through the hands-on activities in each lab.

- **Review Questions:** Questions help reinforce concepts presented in the lab.

Note for instructors: Answers to review questions are available on the Course Technology Web site at *www.course.com*. Search on this book's ISBN, which is shown on the back cover.

HARDWARE REQUIREMENTS

This section lists the hardware required to complete the labs in the book. Many of the individual labs require less hardware than listed below.

- Three computers with Pentium 166-MHz CPU or higher processors (550 MHz recommended) with the following features:
  - 128 MB of RAM minimum (256 MB recommended) in each computer
  - A 4-GB hard disk with at least 1 GB of available storage space (10-GB hard disk or larger with at least 7 GB of available storage space recommended) in each computer
  - A CD-ROM drive
- Internet access
- Two PCI Ethernet network interface cards for each PC
- A hub or switch
- At least 4 Category 5 UTP straight-through patch cables
- At least 2 Category 5 UTP crossover patch cables
- A Cisco Aironet 350 wireless access point (optional)

SOFTWARE/SETUP REQUIREMENTS

- At least two copies of Windows Server 2003
- Internet Explorer 6 Web browser
- ZDelete Disk Wiper*
- Restorer2000*
- Snort 2.1.x*
- WinPcap*
- IDSCenter*
- BackOfficer*

*You can download these programs from the vendors' Web sites. These lab exercises were written using the latest version of the software available at the time of printing. Please note that software versions are subject to change without notice, and any changes could render some activity steps inoperable. Instructors may want to download these programs at the beginning of the course, and store them for future use to ensure that the software corresponds to the activity steps.

Classroom Setup Guidelines

Instructor PC

1. Partitions
   a. C:\ 3-GB NTFS
   b. E:\ 4-GB FAT32

2. Windows Server 2003 Installation
   a. Boot to the Windows Server 2003 CD.
   b. Press F8 to accept the license agreement.
   c. Create a 3-GB partition.
   d. Format the partition using NTFS.
   e. Set Regional settings if necessary.
   f. Enter your name and company.
   g. Enter the Product key.
   h. Select Per Seat licensing.
   i. Computer Name: Instructor
   j. Administrator Password: Pa$$word
   k. Adjust the time zone if necessary.
   l. To establish custom network settings, configure TCP/IP settings with the following:
      i. IP address: 192.168.X.100 (Note: Replace X with the classroom number)
      ii. Subnet mask: 255.255.255.0
      iii. DNS server: 192.168.X.100
      iv. Accept WORKGROUP as the Workgroup.

3. Active Directory setup
   a. Run dcpromo.
   b. Create a new domain and forest.
   c. Let the Active Directory installation install DNS.
   d. DNS name: Class.dom
   e. Accept the default settings (enter "password" for the restore password).

4. DNS setup
   a. Enable dynamic updates on the Class.dom Zone.
   b. Create a standard primary reverse lookup zone for 192.168.x.
   c. DHCP setup
   d. Scope name: Class
   e. IP range: 192.168.X.1–254
   f. Subnet mask: 255.255.255.0
   g. Exclusions: 192.168.X.1–20, 192.168.X.100–254
   h. Configure Options
      i. Router: 192.168.X.100
      ii. Domain name: Class.dom
      iii. DNS server: 192.168.X.100

Student PC

1. Partitions
   a. C:\ 3-GB NTFS
   b. E:\ 4-GB FAT32

2. Windows Server 2003 Installation
   a. Boot to the Windows Server 2003 CD.
   b. Press F8 to accept the license agreement.
   c. Create a 3-GB partition.
   d. Format the partition using NTFS.
   e. Set Regional settings if necessary.
   f. Enter your name and company.
   g. Enter the Product key.
   h. Select Per Seat licensing.
   i. Computer Name: Server-X (Note: Replace X with a number assigned by your instructor)
   j. Administrator Password: Pa$$word
   k. Adjust the time zone if necessary.
   l. Accept the typical network settings.

ACKNOWLEDGMENTS

I would like to thank Course Technology for giving me the opportunity to write the second edition of this lab manual. I also thank everyone on the Security+ team for working well together to meet all deadlines. Thank you Dan Seiter, Amy Lyon, Will Pitkin, Mark Ciampa, Brooke Booth, Christian Kunciw, Chris Scriver, and Shawn Day. Thanks also to the peer reviewers, who worked under very tight deadlines and provided great feedback:

Randy Weaver   Everest College

Shahed Mustafa   Long Island Business Institute

Kelly Cannon   Piedmont Virginia Community College

I'd also like to thank my three boys, Mark, Michael, and Adam, for being such great kids. Finally, I thank Tracy, who amazed me with an endless supply of ice-cold cherry Coke and happiness.

INFORMATION SECURITY FUNDAMENTALS

Labs included in this chapter:

➤ Lab 1.1 Risk Analysis—Definition of Assets

➤ Lab 1.2 Risk Analysis—Threat Assessment

➤ Lab 1.3 Risk Analysis—Risk Assessment

➤ Lab 1.4 Risk Analysis—Recommendations

CompTIA Security+ Exam Objectives	
Objective	Lab
Operational/Organizational Security: Risk Assessment	1.1, 1.2, 1.3, 1.4

LAB 1.1 RISK ANALYSIS—DEFINITION OF ASSETS

Background

You are an IT manager for Acme Books, an e-commerce company that competes with *Amazon.com*. You are trying to justify the implementation of security and disaster recovery upgrades. Acme Books has 5,000 employees with three North American offices in New York, Los Angeles, and Montreal, and two overseas offices in London and Paris. You recently experienced problems with the hardware and software used to run the e-commerce site. These problems resulted in 15 hours of downtime during prime business hours. Upper management sent you a message asking you to explain why the problems occurred and encouraging you to prevent these events in the future. You feel that it is a good time to perform a risk analysis for the company.

Objectives

The first step in risk analysis is to identify all of the assets in the company that may be subject to risk. This can be a difficult and time-consuming process, but it is required for an accurate assessment. Before you can begin a definition of assets, it is important that a recent inventory has been taken. The absence of this inventory could delay the start of a risk analysis project.

After completing this lab, you will be able to:

➤ Define assets

➤ Understand the importance of defining assets

Materials Required

This lab requires the following:

➤ Internet access

Estimated completion time: 20 minutes

ACTIVITY

Document the following assets for Acme Books. Be thorough and creative, because the next three labs build on this one. Feel free to use the Internet for assistance.

1. Document Acme's data/information assets. Examples include:
    - Company data
    - Customer databases
    - Company records
    - Hardcopy printouts, records, legal documents
    - Reference and training materials
    - Billing records

2. Document Acme's software assets. Examples include:
    - Commercial software products
    - Custom-developed application software
    - Database management software
    - Operating systems
    - Network software

3. Document Acme's hardware assets. Examples include:
    - Mainframes, minicomputers, and microcomputers
    - Disk and tape drives
    - Printers
    - Terminals
    - Fax machines
    - Modems
    - Power supplies
    - Communications devices (routers, controllers, and so on)

Certification Objectives

Objectives for CompTIA Security+ Exam:

➤ Operational/Organizational Security: Risk Assessment

Review Questions

1. Which of the following are considered data/information?
    a. terminals
    b. operating systems
    c. company records
    d. commercial software products

2. Database management software fits into which of the following categories?

   a. data/information

   b. software

   c. hardware

   d. all of the above

3. Databases fit into which of the following categories?

   a. data/information

   b. software

   c. hardware

   d. all of the above

4. An accurate inventory is important when performing a risk assessment. True or False?

5. Hardcopy printouts are not important if electronic copies are available. True or False?

LAB 1.2 RISK ANALYSIS—THREAT ASSESSMENT

Objectives

Once you have identified a company's assets, you can begin to evaluate the potential threats to them. Knowing the potential consequences of any threatening event is crucial to the overall process of risk assessment. To begin this process, you must identify the possible events and classify them. Then you must determine the likelihood that each event will occur, and the impact of each event. Finally, you must determine the consequences of the event and how the company would be affected. This last determination may be the most important item for management when considering a contingency for each threat.

After completing this lab, you will be able to:

➤ Perform a threat assessment

➤ Understand the importance of threat assessments

Materials Required

This lab requires the following:

➤ Internet access

Estimated completion time: 20 minutes

LAB ACTIVITY

ACTIVITY

1. For each asset you identified in Lab 1.1, identify the potential agents or events that could place the asset at risk. Consider the following examples.
   - Theft
   - Vandalism
   - Fire
   - Flood
   - Power loss
   - Unauthorized access
   - Viruses
   - Corruption of data

2. Classify each agent or event by the following types of threats:
   - Disclosure
   - Interruption
   - Modification
   - Removal
   - Destruction

3. Classify the likelihood of each agent or event as one of the following:
   - Low—There is no history, and the threat is unlikely to occur.
   - Medium—There is some history, and an assessment has been made that the threat may occur.
   - High—There is significant history, and an assessment has been made that the threat is quite likely to occur.

4. Rate the impact of each possible event as one of the following:
   - Very serious (may compromise the entire business)
   - Serious (may disrupt normal operations, cause significant inconvenience to clients, or be costly to rectify)
   - Less serious (may disrupt noncritical operations or cause limited inconvenience to employees)

5. Identify the potential consequences as one of the following:
   - Loss of privacy
   - Loss of trust
   - Loss of asset
   - Loss of service

Certification Objectives

Objectives for CompTIA Security+ Exam:

➤ Operational/Organizational Security: Risk Assessment

Review Questions

1. An event that may disrupt normal business operations would be classified as
   _____ .
   a. very serious
   b. serious
   c. less serious

2. An event that is classified as having significant history is considered to have a
   _____ likelihood of occurring.
   a. low
   b. medium
   c. high

3. An event that may disrupt noncritical business operations and cause employee
   inconvenience would be _____ .
   a. very serious
   b. serious
   c. less serious

4. An event that is classified as having no history is considered to have a
   _____ likelihood of occurring.
   a. low
   b. medium
   c. high

5. Which of the following are potential consequences of an event?

   a. loss of asset

   b. loss of privacy

   c. loss of trust

   d. loss of service

   e. all of the above

LAB 1.3 RISK ANALYSIS—RISK ASSESSMENT

Objectives

At this point you must evaluate a company's existing safeguards to see what assets have not been protected. Most companies have some safeguards in place, but they are usually minimal. You may want to consider a compare-and-contrast approach to risk assessment. It is also important to research examples of how other similar companies are handling risk.

After completing this lab, you will be able to:

➤ Perform a risk assessment

➤ Understand the importance of risk assessments

Materials Required

This lab requires the following:

➤ Internet access

Estimated completion time: 20 minutes

LAB ACTIVITY

ACTIVITY

In this activity you assess the adequacy of the company's existing safeguards to protect against potential threats.

1. List the existing safeguards that protect against a potential event. For example, the company may have after-hours security and surveillance cameras installed at all entrances to the facility to protect against theft or vandalism, or access security already built into the present system to protect against computer hackers.

2. In consideration of existing safeguards, is the company still vulnerable to the possible threat? Describe the vulnerability. In other words, how can a threat or threat agent attack the asset being protected?

3. What is the risk to the company of the event occurring?

NOTE

Risk refers to the company's ability to protect itself in the face of the event occurring, not to the likelihood of the event happening.

4. Rate the potential risk as:
   - Low—Requires some attention and consideration for safeguard implementation as good business practice
   - Moderate—Requires attention and safeguard implementation in the near future
   - High—Requires immediate attention and safeguard implementation

Certification Objectives

Objectives for CompTIA Security+ Exam:

➤ Operational/Organizational Security: Risk Assessment

Review Questions

1. A company puts a _____ in place to protect against an attack.
   a. risk
   b. safeguard
   c. vulnerability
   d. threat

2. Risk refers to a company's ability to protect itself from the likelihood of an event occurring. True or False?

3. A _____ is considered a breakdown in company protection.
   a. risk
   b. safeguard
   c. vulnerability
   d. threat

4. Which of the following are considered safeguards?
   a. after-hours security
   b. surveillance cameras
   c. firewalls
   d. all of the above

5. Which level of potential risk requires attention and safeguard implementation in the near future?

   a. high

   b. moderate

   c. low

   d. none of the above

LAB 1.4 RISK ANALYSIS—RECOMMENDATIONS

Objectives

After you have performed the definition of assets, threat assessment, and risk assessment, you can make some recommendations to management. First you must develop a proposal that documents the specific risks to the company. After presenting the risks, you can recommend safeguards to reduce the risk.

After completing this lab, you will be able to:

➤ Develop risk analysis recommendations

➤ Understand the importance of risk analysis recommendations

Materials Required

This lab requires the following:

➤ Internet access

Estimated completion time: 20 minutes

ACTIVITY

1. In consideration of the potential vulnerability and risk, what additional safeguards are recommended to lower the risk to an acceptable level? Describe the proposed measures.

NOTE
There may be a number of alternative safeguards, providing different levels of protection, that may be selected based on the availability of resources, acceptable level of risk, and so forth.

2. For the proposed safeguards, rate the projected risk for each as one of the following:

- Low
- Moderate
- High

NOTE After ranking the safeguards, it is not always practical to implement all the high-risk solutions because of technical or physical limitations, time constraints, or financial constraints.

Certification Objectives

Objectives for CompTIA Security+ Exam:

➤ Operational/Organizational Security: Risk Assessment

Review Questions

1. Why should you rank safeguards?

   a. Management will never approve the safeguard with the highest cost.

   b. It is not always practical to implement all solutions.

   c. You may have to use a phased approach.

   d. Ranking can keep you organized.

2. A certain amount of risk is considered acceptable. True or False?

3. Safeguards might have to be eliminated from consideration for which of the following reasons?

   a. physical limitations

   b. financial constraints

   c. technical limitations

   d. all of the above

4. A projected risk must be based on the past experience of another company. True or False?

5. Alternatives to safeguards are important because of _____ .

   a. availability of resources

   b. acceptable level of risk

   c. different levels of protection

   d. all of the above

CHAPTER TWO

ATTACKERS AND THEIR ATTACKS

Labs included in this chapter:

➤ Lab 2.1 Using the At Command to Start System Processes
➤ Lab 2.2 Researching DoS and DDoS Attacks
➤ Lab 2.3 Researching the CPUHOG DoS Attack
➤ Lab 2.4 Researching the NetBus Trojan Horse
➤ Lab 2.5 Removing NetBus from an Infected System

CompTIA Security+ Exam Objectives	
Objective	Lab
General Security Concepts: Attacks: DoS/DDoS	2.2, 2.3
General Security Concepts: Malicious Code: Trojan Horses	2.1, 2.4, 2.5

LAB 2.1 USING THE AT COMMAND TO START SYSTEM PROCESSES

Objectives

One shortcoming of the Windows operating system is that it lacks the ability to execute a program on a remote system. If you connect to a server and double-click an executable file, it runs on your system. Windows Resource Kit utilities are available to assist with this shortcoming, but another method works well. Using the "at" command, you can schedule an executable file to run on a remote system at a specific time. This is a common method used to install Trojan horses.

After completing this lab, you will be able to:

➤ Use the at command to execute remote programs

➤ Find individual system processes and stop them

Materials Required

This lab requires the following:

➤ Windows Server 2003 servers working in groups of two

➤ Administrator access to both servers

> Estimated completion time: 30 minutes

ACTIVITY

The servers used in this activity are called Server-X and Server-Y. Please substitute the names of your own servers.

1. On Server-X, log on as Administrator.

2. Press **Ctrl+Alt+Del**.

3. Click **Task Manager**.

4. Click the **Processes** tab and make a note of the current processes. (*Hint*: Look for notepad.exe. You should not see it.) When you finish, close Task Manager.

5. On Server-Y, log on as Administrator.

6. Click **Start**, click **All Programs**, click **Accessories**, and then click **Command Prompt**. Type **cd** and press **Enter**.

7. At the command line, type **net time \\server-x** and then press **Enter**. This command tells you the current time for Server-X so you can schedule the execution of a program.

Server-X should be your partner's server name, Server-Y should be your server name, and the time should be the current time.

8. At the command line, type **at \\server-x 1:58p /interactive "notepad.exe"** and then press **Enter**. Note that you should replace "1:58p" with a time that is three minutes later than the current time on your Server-X.

9. Type **at \\server-x** to see the scheduled task. These steps are illustrated in Figure 2-1. At the specified time, Notepad starts on Server-X.

```
Command Prompt                                              _|□|×|
Microsoft Windows [Version 5.2.3790]
(C) Copyright 1985-2003 Microsoft Corp.

C:\Documents and Settings\Administrator>cd\

C:\>net time \\server-x
Current time at \\server-x is 2/11/2004 1:55 PM

The command completed successfully.

C:\>at \\server-x 1:58p /interactive "notepad.exe"
Added a new job with job ID = 1

C:\>at \\server-x
Status ID   Day                    Time          Command Line
--------------------------------------------------------------------
        1   Today                  1:58 PM       notepad.exe

C:\>
```

Figure 2-1 The at command used in Notepad

10. If you want to start a process that is hidden from your partner, repeat Step 8 but remove the /interactive switch, as follows: **at \\server-x 1:58p "notepad.exe"**.

11. Switch to Server-X after the time you specified in Step 8 has passed. Notice that the Notepad window is open on Server-X. Press **Ctrl+Alt+Del**.

12. Open **Task Manager**.

13. Click the **Processes** tab and look for **notepad.exe**, as shown in Figure 2-2.

14. Close all open windows on Server-X and Server-Y.

The application was executed on Server-X. If you completed Step 10, the application was executed but did not appear on the Server-X screen.

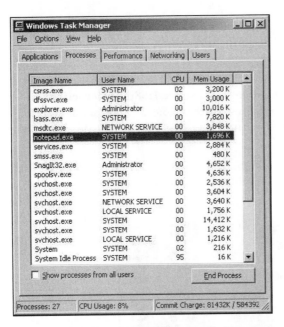

Figure 2-2 Notepad in Windows Task Manager

Certification Objectives

Objectives for CompTIA Security+ Exam:

➤ General Security Concepts: Malicious Code: Trojan Horses

Review Questions

1. Which of the following best describes the at command?

   a. a program that can execute commands and other programs needed to install program updates

   b. a program that can schedule commands and other programs to run on a computer at a specific time and date

   c. a Resource Kit utility that can schedule commands and programs to run on a computer at a specific time and date

   d. a Trojan horse that can schedule commands and programs to run on a computer at a specific time and date

2

2. What switch allows the user to see the process that started with the at command?

   a. /delete

   b. /interaction

   c. /interactive

   d. /visible

3. Which of the following is a legitimate use for the at command?

   a. scheduling backups

   b. scheduling virus scans

   c. scheduling updates

   d. all of the above

4. What is the result of the following command: at \\server-x 3:25 "notepad"?

   a. A Notepad process will start on Server-X immediately.

   b. A Notepad process will start on Server-X at 3:25 p.m.

   c. A Notepad process will start on Server-X at 3:25 a.m.

   d. Nothing, the command was incorrectly entered.

5. What is the result of the following command: at \\server-y 14 /delete?

   a. Scheduled id 14 will be deleted from the schedule on Server-Y.

   b. Scheduled id 14 will be deleted from the schedule on Server-X.

   c. Scheduled id 14 will be added to the schedule on Server-X.

   d. Scheduled id 14 will be deleted from the schedule on the local system.

LAB 2.2 RESEARCHING DoS AND DDoS ATTACKS

Objectives

Hackers are not always interested in gaining access to resources and stealing information. Sometimes they just want to entertain themselves by preventing a company from doing business online. This is called a denial-of-service attack, or DoS. There are many ways to cause a DoS, but the general idea is to overload a system so that it cannot respond to legitimate customers. One of TCP/IP's useful utilities, ping, can be used in a malicious way to cause a DoS. If you ping a system with an IP address, it replies. The idea behind using the ping utility to cause a DoS attack is to bombard a system with Internet Control Message Protocol (ICMP) packets used by ping, so that the system cannot respond to legitimate requests. In this case, hackers may use a distributed DoS (DDoS), in which multiple machines work together to perform the attack.

After completing this lab, you will be able to:

➤ Understand how a DoS attack works

Materials Required

This lab requires the following:

➤ A Windows Server 2003 server with Internet access

Estimated completion time: 30 minutes

LAB ACTIVITY

ACTIVITY

1. Search the Internet for "Denial of Service" and "Distributed Denial of Service." You can find comprehensive descriptions on the CERT Coordination Center Web site: *www.cert.org/tech_tips/denial_of_service.html*.

2. List five different methods of starting a DoS or DDoS attack.

3. Document the history of DoS and DDoS attacks.

4. Describe the effects of a DoS or DDoS attack.

Certification Objectives

Objectives for CompTIA Security+ Exam:

➤ General Security Concepts: Attacks: DoS/DDoS

Review Questions

1. What does ICMP stand for?
   a. Internet Computer Management Protocol
   b. Internet Control Management Protocol
   c. Internet Control Message Protocol
   d. Internet Computer Message Protocol

2. Which of the following is a program that uses ICMP?
   a. DNS
   b. FTP
   c. Telnet
   d. ping

3. What kind of attack uses multiple computers to attack another computer?
   a. denial of service
   b. denial of system
   c. distributed denial of system
   d. distributed denial of service

4. Which of the following sends packets to a destination but never completes the third step of the TCP handshake?
   a. DoS
   b. SYN snoop
   c. SYN flood
   d. SYN flop

5. A hacker modifies the source address of a packet so it appears to be a different host. This is known as which of the following?
   a. spoofing
   b. faking
   c. spooling
   d. masking

LAB 2.3 RESEARCHING THE CPUHOG DoS ATTACK

Objectives

The three most important resources for a computer are memory, storage, and processor power. If you take any of the three away, the system is useless. The CPUHOG attack consumes most of a processor's resources and causes a DoS by setting the process priority level to the highest level possible, which is 16. Windows will try to fix this problem, but it can only increase an application's priority to 15. As you may guess, CPUHOG will always have priority over other applications, including Task Manager. This could require a cold boot to restore the system's functionality.

After completing this lab, you will be able to:

➤ Understand processor resources and priority

➤ Describe the impact CPUHOG can have on a system

Materials Required

This lab requires the following:

➤ A Windows Server 2003 server with Internet access

Estimated completion time: **30 minutes**

ACTIVITY

1. Search the Internet for "CPUHOG."

2. Write a short summary describing a CPUHOG.

3. Search the Internet for "Windows application priorities."

4. Write a short summary explaining Windows system application and process priorities.

5. Describe the impact that a CPUHOG attack can have on a server.

Certification Objectives

Objectives for CompTIA Security+ Exam:

➤ General Security Concepts: Attacks: DoS/DDoS

Review Questions

1. Which of the following is the most important computer resource?

    a. processor

    b. disk space

    c. memory

    d. all of the above

2. How many priority levels are available in Windows NT?

    a. 1

    b. 32

    c. 16

    d. 15

3. What is the highest priority that Windows NT can give an application?

    a. 1

    b. 32

    c. 16

    d. 15

4. What best describes CPUHOG?

    a. a program that consumes most of the processor's resources

    b. a program that consumes most of the memory's resources

    c. a program that consumes most of the hard drive's resources

    d. a program that consumes most of the computer's resources

5. CPUHOG is successful in a DoS because Windows allows applications to set their own priority. True or False?

LAB 2.4 RESEARCHING THE NETBUS TROJAN HORSE

Objectives

Another goal of a hacker is to gain access to a system without the user's knowledge. Programs that allow this type of access are called Trojan horses. A Trojan horse is a program that may seem desirable, but is actually harmful. One of the best-known Trojan horses is NetBus. NetBus was created in 1998 as a remote administration tool, with some additional fun tools and games. These tools could be used to redirect ports, start applications, and even view the screen of a remote user. NetBus was distributed to some unsuspecting users with a game called Whack-a-Mole, which then became a Trojan horse on the users' hard drives. The users thought they had a fun game to play, but it was actually a harmful program. Users also forwarded the game to their friends, which only compounded the problem. Today, most virus detection software prevents NetBus from successfully attacking a system.

After completing this lab, you will be able to:

➤ Understand the impact Trojan horses have on networks

➤ Describe the origins and effects of the NetBus Trojan horse

Materials Required

This lab requires the following:

➤ A Windows Server 2003 server with Internet access

Estimated completion time: 30 minutes

ACTIVITY

1. Search the Internet for "NetBus Trojan horse."

2. Write a one-page summary of the history of NetBus.

3. List the different versions of NetBus and the features associated with each version.

_____

_____

4. Explain the difference between the client and server components of NetBus.

_____

_____

5. Describe the effects of the NetBus Trojan horse.

_____

_____

Certification Objectives

Objectives for CompTIA Security+ Exam:

➤ General Security Concepts: Malicious Code: Trojan Horses

Review Questions

1. Which of the following best describes a Trojan horse?
   a. a program that requires a host program to run
   b. a program that does something other than what it appears to be intended to do
   c. a program that contains a mistake in the programming code
   d. a self-contained program that can replicate itself

2. Which of the following can help prevent the spread of Trojan horses? (Choose all that apply.)
   a. firewall
   b. virus scanner
   c. program debugger
   d. router

3. Which of the following ports is commonly associated with NetBus?
   a. 31337
   b. 65000
   c. 1024
   d. 12345

4. Which of the following are components of NetBus? (Choose all that apply.)

    a. dynamic libraries

    b. directory

    c. client

    d. server

5. Which of the following can NetBus accomplish? (Choose all that apply.)

    a. switch mouse buttons

    b. start applications

    c. capture screens

    d. redirect ports

LAB 2.5 REMOVING NETBUS FROM AN INFECTED SYSTEM

Objectives

The following lab can be useful if you have been infected with the NetBus Trojan horse. All recent virus detection software can prevent NetBus from attacking a system, but the programs do not do a good job of removing it. With each release of NetBus, it becomes more difficult to remove. This lab contains all of the necessary steps to remove NetBus version 1.7. If your system is not infected, this lab can be a good tool for your network security toolbox. Use the Internet to research how to remove other versions of this Trojan horse.

After completing this lab, you will be able to:

➤ Determine if NetBus is installed on a system

➤ Remove NetBus from a system and prevent future attacks

Materials Required

This lab requires the following:

➤ A Windows Server 2003 server

➤ Administrator access to the server

➤ Completion of Lab 2.4

➤ A PC infected with the NetBus Trojan horse (optional)

Estimated completion time: 15–30 minutes

ACTIVITY

1. Log on to the server as Administrator.

2. Click **Start** and then click **Search**. In the **All or part of the file name** field, enter the file names in the following steps.

Some of the files listed in Step 3 through Step 8 may not exist.

3. Search for **patch.exe** and delete any results.

4. Search for **rundll.dll** and delete any results.

Do not delete rundll32.exe.

5. Search for **keyhook.dl_** and delete any results.

6. Search for **keyhook.dll** and delete any results.

7. Search for **nbsetup1.reg** and delete any results.

8. Search for **nbsetup2.reg** and delete any results.

9. Close the Search window.

10. Click **Start**, click **Run**, type **Regedit**, and then press **Enter**.

11. Navigate to **HKEY_LOCAL_MACHINE\SOFTWARE\ Microsoft\Windows\CurrentVersion\Run**.

12. Delete the key name **PATCH**. The value of the key should be C:\Windows\patch.exe /nomsg.

It is possible for NetBus to use a different name than patch.exe, but it always ends with /nomsg (see Figure 2-3).

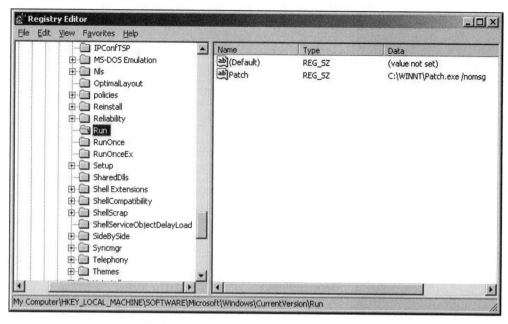

Figure 2-3 Removing NetBus from a system

13. Delete the keys referring to **rundll** and **rundll32** if they exist.

14. Reboot the computer; NetBus will be gone. At this point you should check the "at" schedule and install a virus program to protect the system.

Certification Objectives

Objectives for CompTIA Security+ Exam:

➤ General Security Concepts: Malicious Code: Trojan Horses

Review Questions

1. Which version of NetBus allows the default port to be changed?

    a. 1.20

    b. 1.50

    c. 1.60

    d. 1.70

2. Which Trojan horse is similar to NetBus?

    a. BackOffice

    b. BackOrifice

    c. BackBacon

    d. BackUps

3. Which of the following are games known to be associated with NetBus? (Choose all that apply.)

    a. Hack-a-Mole

    b. Whack-a-Mole

    c. Whackjob

    d. Whackmole

4. The removal process for NetBus is different depending on the version. True or False?

5. Which of the following files is the client portion of NetBus?

    a. netBus.exe

    b. patch.exe

    c. packs.exe

    d. rundll32.exe

CHAPTER THREE

SECURITY BASICS

Labs included in this chapter:

➤ Lab 3.1 Using the Windows Server 2003 Local Password Policy Settings for Length

➤ Lab 3.2 Using the Windows Server 2003 Local Password Policy Settings for Complexity

➤ Lab 3.3 Preventing the Display of the Last Logon Name

➤ Lab 3.4 Setting an Account Lockout Policy

➤ Lab 3.5 Using the Run As Command to Bypass Security

CompTIA Security+ Exam Objectives	
Objective	Lab
General Security Concepts: Authentication: User Name/Password	3.1, 3.2
General Security Concepts: Authentication	3.3, 3.4, 3.5

LAB 3.1 USING THE WINDOWS SERVER 2003 LOCAL PASSWORD POLICY SETTINGS FOR LENGTH

Objectives

Authentication is the process of verifying a person's identity for the purposes of allowing access to a computer system. For authentication to work properly in a networking environment, a user name and password are required. Unfortunately, many people take authentication lightly and do not follow basic security principles. They share passwords with others and sometimes even write passwords down. Enforcing security policies can be difficult, especially for large companies. Another problem with authentication is the length of passwords; short passwords or blank passwords are easier to crack. With this in mind, Windows Server 2003 instituted a local password policy to allow you to specify the minimum length for passwords.

After completing this lab, you will be able to:

➤ Modify the Windows Server 2003 local security policy

➤ Change the "Minimum password length" password policy

Materials Required

This lab requires the following:

➤ A Windows Server 2003 server configured as a stand-alone server

➤ Administrator access to the server

➤ Two user-level accounts: User1 and User2 (each account should have the password set to "password")

> Estimated completion time: 15 minutes

LAB ACTIVITY

ACTIVITY

1. Log on to the Windows Server 2003 server as Administrator.

2. Click **Start**, click **All Programs**, click **Administrative Tools**, and then click **Local Security Policy**.

3. Expand **Account Policies**.

4. Click **Password Policy**. You see a screen that resembles Figure 3-1.

5. Double-click **Minimum password length**.

6. Change the characters value from 0 to **9**, as shown in Figure 3-2.

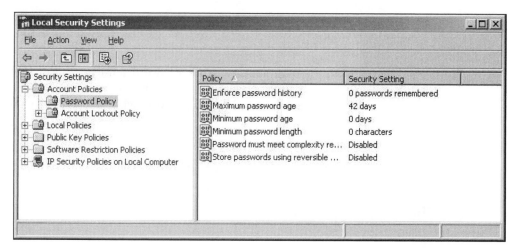

Figure 3-1 Local security settings

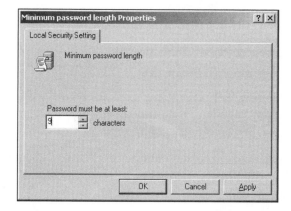

Figure 3-2 Setting the minimum password length

The current password for user accounts is "password." This verifies that the change worked.

NOTE

   7. Click **OK**.

   8. Close all windows and log off.

   9. Log on as User1; Windows allows you to use the existing password.

 10. Press **Ctrl+Alt+Delete**.

 11. Click **Change Password**.

 12. Type **password** for the old password.

13. Type a new password of less than nine characters in both the New Password and Confirm New Password text boxes. Click **OK**. This step is not meant to be successful.

   The following message appears: "Your password must be at least 9 characters, cannot repeat any of your previous 0 passwords, and must be at least 0 days old. Please type a different password. Type a password which meets these requirements in both text boxes."

14. Click **OK** to close the warning window.

15. Try assigning **password1** as the new password. The password change will be successful.

Certification Objectives

Objectives for CompTIA Security+ Exam:

➤   General Security Concepts: Authentication: User Name/Password

Review Questions

1. Which of the following best describes authentication?
   a. the process of gaining access to resources
   b. the process of using resources
   c. the process of verifying the identification of a user
   d. the process of assigning permissions to users

2. Which of the following is required to authenticate to a Windows Server 2003 domain? (Choose all that apply.)
   a. a domain or computer name
   b. a user name
   c. a PIN
   d. a password

3. Why is password length important?
   a. Longer passwords are impossible to hack.
   b. Longer passwords are harder to hack.
   c. Windows requires long passwords in a domain environment.
   d. Longer passwords can prevent password-cracking programs from working properly.

4. By default, what is the minimum password length for Windows Server 2003 computers?
   a. six characters
   b. five characters

        c. eight characters

        d. zero characters

   5. What is the reasoning behind the Windows password length recommendation?

        a. Windows hashes passwords.

        b. Users are less likely to write down a longer password.

        c. Windows crashes passwords.

        d. Windows uses Kerberos for passwords.

3

LAB 3.2 USING THE WINDOWS SERVER 2003 PASSWORD POLICY SETTINGS FOR COMPLEXITY

Objectives

While the length of a password is very important, the complexity of a password is just as important. For example, a password that uses consecutive digits or characters, such as 1234567 or abcdefg, is not very secure; a password-cracking program could crack it in a short amount of time. With the Windows Server 2003 password complexity policy, a user is required to include at least three of the following characters in a password: one number, one uppercase letter, one lowercase letter, and one symbol. Combining password length with complexity is recommended by most security professionals.

After completing this lab, you will be able to:

➤ Modify the Windows Server 2003 local security policy

➤ Change the "Password must meet complexity requirements" password policy

Materials Required

This lab requires the following:

➤ A Windows Server 2003 server configured as a stand-alone server

➤ Administrator access to the server

➤ Two user-level accounts: User1 and User2

Estimated completion time: 15 minutes

LAB ACTIVITY

ACTIVITY

1. Log on to the Windows Server 2003 server as Administrator.

2. Click **Start**, click **All Programs**, click **Administrative Tools**, and then click **Local Security Policy**.

3. Expand **Account Policies**.

4. Click **Password Policy**.

5. Double-click **Password must meet complexity requirements**.

6. Click the **Enabled** option, as shown in Figure 3-3.

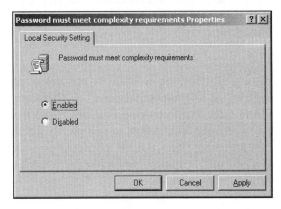

Figure 3-3 Password complexity requirements

7. Click **OK**.

8. Close all windows and log off.

9. Log on as User1; Windows remembers that the password is set as password1.

10. Press **Ctrl+Alt+Delete**.

11. Click **Change Password**.

12. Type **password1** for the old password.

13. Type **password** for the new password in both text boxes, and then click **OK**. The following message appears: "Your password must be at least 9 characters; cannot repeat any of your previous 0 passwords; must be at least 0 days old; must contain capitals, numerals or punctuation; and cannot contain your account or full name. Please type a different password. Type a password which meets these requirements in both text boxes."

14. Click **OK** to close the warning window.

15. Try assigning **Password1** as the new password. The password change will be successful. Note that the old password was password1.

Certification Objectives

Objectives for CompTIA Security+ Exam:

➤ General Security Concepts: Authentication: User Name/Password

Review Questions

1. Why are complex passwords important? (Choose all that apply.)
    a. Complex passwords are more difficult to crack.
    b. The complexity of passwords adds to the security of long passwords.
    c. Complex passwords are impossible to crack.
    d. Complex passwords help users create strong passwords.

2. Which of the following is considered a complex password? (Choose all that apply.)
    a. @1c4htj3
    b. Pa$$w0rd
    c. ncdjszkjdnc
    d. Ajd649sg

3. Even though you have implemented the recommended password length and complexity policy, applications such as FTP and Telnet are not recommended for remote connections for which of the following reasons?
    a. FTP and Telnet require Kerberos.
    b. FTP and Telnet cannot use special characters in passwords.
    c. FTP and Telnet send passwords in plain text.
    d. FTP and Telnet have security exploits.

4. Which authentication protocol(s) that can encrypt passwords can be used with Windows Server 2003? (Choose all that apply.)
    a. CHAP
    b. PAP
    c. SPAP
    d. EAP

5. Which of the following is a remote access authentication protocol? (Choose all that apply.)
    a. CHAP
    b. SPA
    c. PAP
    d. MS-CHAP

LAB 3.3 PREVENTING THE DISPLAY OF THE LAST LOGON NAME

Objectives

One way to discourage a password hacker is to remove the name of the last user to log on from the Log On to Windows entry window. This is especially useful on remote-access computers. Without an account name, the hacker will have an extra step to complete before gaining access to the system. Otherwise, the hacker will know at least one account on the system and will only have to crack the password. If someone has physical access to a computer, cracking passwords can be relatively easy.

After completing this lab, you will be able to:

➤ Modify the Windows Server 2003 local security policy

➤ Change the "Do not display last user name" security option

Materials Required

This lab requires the following:

➤ A Windows Server 2003 server configured as a stand-alone server

➤ Administrator access to the server

➤ Two user-level accounts: User1 and User2

Estimated completion time: 15 minutes

ACTIVITY

1. Log on to the Windows Server 2003 server as Administrator.

2. Click **Start**, click **All Programs**, click **Administrative Tools**, and then click **Local Security Policy**.

3. Expand **Local Policies**.

4. Click **Security Options**. A screen resembling Figure 3-4 appears.

5. Double-click **Interactive logon: Do not display last user name**.

6. Click the **Enabled** option, as shown in Figure 3-5.

7. Click **OK**.

8. Close all windows and log off.

9. Press **Ctrl+Alt+Delete**. Notice that the User name field is empty in the logon screen.

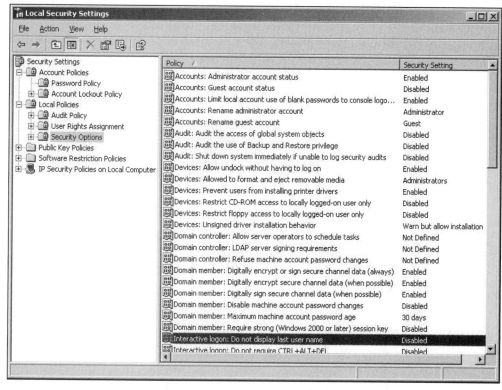

Figure 3-4 Security settings

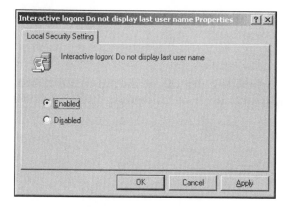

Figure 3-5 Enabling interactive logon

Certification Objectives

Objectives for CompTIA Security+ Exam:

➤ General Security Concepts: Authentication

Review Questions

1. What is the advantage of removing the name of the last user to log on?

    a. allows users to share computers

    b. requires users to remember their user names

    c. requires a hacker to take an extra step when cracking passwords

    d. hides the identity of the Windows domain

2. Which default Windows NT/2003 account should be renamed to assist this method of authentication protection?

    a. Domain Admins

    b. Domain Guests

    c. Administrator

    d. Guest

3. Which account should be disabled to assist this method of authentication protection?

    a. Guest

    b. Administrator

    c. User1

    d. User2

4. Who can delete the Guest account?

    a. no one

    b. Administrator

    c. Domain Admins

    d. Guest

5. Biometrics is an additional method that can be used to secure authentication. Which of the following is an example of a biometric device? (Choose all that apply.)

    a. complex passwords

    b. fingerprints

    c. retinal scans

    d. smart cards

LAB 3.4 SETTING AN ACCOUNT LOCKOUT POLICY

3

Objectives

Another measure you can take to create a roadblock for hackers is to implement an account lockout policy. Hackers who have the time and patience can crack any password. An account lockout policy disables an account for a specific amount of time after a certain number of failed logon attempts. This can help delay a successful hack attempt or, better yet, discourage the hacker from continuing.

After completing this lab, you will be able to:

➤ Modify the Windows Server 2003 local security policy

➤ Change the "Account lockout threshold" account lockout policy

➤ Change the "Reset account lockout counter" account lockout policy

Materials Required

This lab requires the following:

➤ A Windows Server 2003 server configured as a stand-alone server

➤ Administrator access to the server

➤ Two user-level accounts: User1 and User2

Estimated completion time: 20 minutes

LAB ACTIVITY

ACTIVITY

1. Log on to the Windows Server 2003 server as Administrator.

2. Click **Start**, click **All Programs**, click **Administrative Tools**, and then click **Local Security Policy**.

3. Expand **Account Policies**.

4. Click **Account Lockout Policy**. A screen resembling Figure 3-6 appears.

5. Double-click **Account lockout threshold**.

6. Change the invalid logon attempts to **3**, as shown in Figure 3-7.

7. Click **OK**.

8. You are prompted to change the values for the Account lockout duration and Reset account lockout counter after policies, as shown in Figure 3-8.

9. Click **OK** to accept the changes and notice how the Security settings changed, as shown in Figure 3-9.

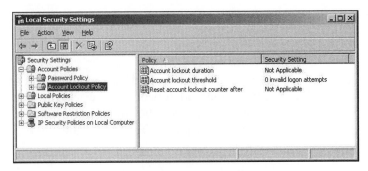

Figure 3-6 Setting the account lockout policy

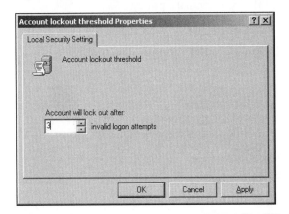

Figure 3-7 Setting the account lockout threshold

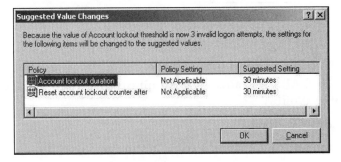

Figure 3-8 Prompt to change lockout values

10. Close all windows and log off.

11. Log on as User2 to verify that the account is functional. The password is "password."

12. Log off User2 and try to log on three times without entering a password.

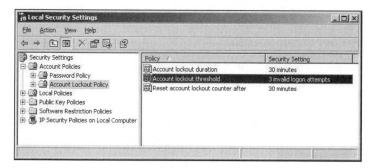

Figure 3-9 Noting changes to lockout settings

13. Try to log on a fourth time. The following message appears: "Unable to log you on because your account has been locked out, please contact your administrator."

14. Click **OK**.

15. You can now either wait 30 minutes or log on as Administrator and unlock the account, as shown in Figure 3-10, by right-clicking the user account in the Local Users and Groups extension of the Computer Management snap-in under Administrative Tools.

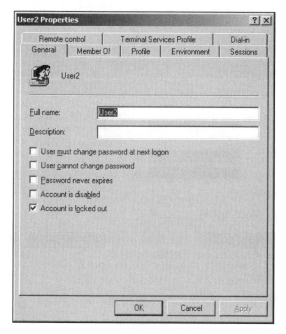

Figure 3-10 Unlocking the account

Certification Objectives

Objectives for CompTIA Security+ Exam:

➤ General Security Concepts: Authentication

Review Questions

1. Why is it important to implement an account lockout policy?
    a. prevents users from forgetting passwords
    b. prevents hackers from hacking continuously
    c. forces users to write down passwords
    d. creates a log of hack attempts

2. Which settings can be configured in the Windows Server 2003 account lockout policy? (Choose all that apply.)
    a. account lockout threshold
    b. account lockout duration
    c. account lockout length
    d. reset account lockout counter after

3. Which feature of the account lockout policy can be used to assist account operators when handling locked-out accounts?
    a. account lockout threshold
    b. account lockout duration
    c. account lockout length
    d. reset account lockout counter after

4. How can an administrator access a system once the Administrator account has been locked out and a reset counter has not been set?
    a. Restore the account database from a backup.
    b. The Administrator account cannot be locked out.
    c. Restart the computer.
    d. The system will be inaccessible.

5. If you implement an account lockout and reset counter policy, how can you monitor the failed attempts? (Choose all that apply.)
    a. Enable Account Policies.
    b. Check the System log in Event Viewer.
    c. Enable Auditing.
    d. Check the Security log in Event Viewer.

LAB 3.5 USING THE RUN AS COMMAND TO BYPASS SECURITY

Objectives

Before the explosion of e-mail viruses, many network administrators used their administrative account to complete daily tasks such as composing memos and checking e-mail. After the I Love You virus was released and wreaked havoc on numerous network files, most companies required administrators to use two accounts. One account was for administrative tasks, and the other was for day-to-day tasks. While this practice is more secure, it is very inconvenient. Many administrators did what they could to find ways around this policy, including ignoring it. Windows Server 2003 has a feature, the Run As command, which fixes this problem. The command allows an administrator to log on with a standard user account and still run administrative programs with administrative rights. Those rights are only applied to the application, so viruses, worms, and Trojan horses cannot access the network with administrative privileges.

After completing this lab, you will be able to:

➤ Identify Run As procedures

➤ Run programs as Administrator while logged on as a regular user

Materials Required

This lab requires the following:

➤ A Windows Server 2003 server configured as a stand-alone server

➤ Administrator access to the server

➤ Two user-level accounts: User1 and User2

Estimated completion time: 15 minutes

ACTIVITY

1. Log on as User2. The password is "password."

2. Click **Start**, click **Control Panel**, and then click **Administrative Tools**. The error message shown in Figure 3-11 appears.

3. Click **Close**.

4. Right-click the **Local Security Policy** icon.

5. Click **Run As**.

6. Enter the necessary Administrator account information. An example is shown in Figure 3-12.

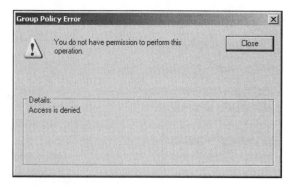

Figure 3-11 Policy error

Figure 3-12 Run As window

7. Click **OK**. You can now edit the Local Security Policy. Close all open windows.

Certification Objectives

Objectives for CompTIA Security+ Exam:

➤   General Security Concepts: Authentication

Review Questions

1. Which of the following is an advantage of using the Run As command?
    a. allows users to bypass security without permission
    b. helps prevent the spread of viruses
    c. conserves resources for administrators
    d. allows administrators to check e-mail and administer the network

2. Which of the following is a disadvantage of the Run As command? (Choose all that apply.)
    a. opens potential security holes
    b. allows users to install applications if they know the local administrator password
    c. allows users to access administrative tools if they know the local administrator password
    d. allows users to change account permissions

3. How can you use the Run As command on an existing shortcut?
    a. Right-click the shortcut.
    b. Hold down the Alt key and right-click the shortcut.
    c. Hold down the Shift key and right-click the shortcut.
    d. Hold down the Ctrl key and right-click the shortcut.

4. What application should you not use the Run As command to execute?
    a. a virus scanner
    b. an e-mail application
    c. a word processor
    d. an auditing program

5. How can you prevent users from using the Run As command?
    a. Delete the Run As command.
    b. Disable the Secondary Logon service.
    c. Disable the Server service.
    d. Delete the RunAs.dll file.

CHAPTER FOUR

SECURITY BASELINES

Labs included in this chapter:

➤ Lab 4.1 Defining Security Templates in Windows Server 2003

➤ Lab 4.2 Managing Windows Server 2003 Security Templates

➤ Lab 4.3 Protecting the System Accounts Database

➤ Lab 4.4 Configuring Services and Processes

➤ Lab 4.5 Configuring Network Settings

CompTIA Security+ Exam Objectives	
Objective	Lab
Infrastructure Security: Security Baselines	4.1, 4.2
Infrastructure Security: Devices	4.3, 4.4, 4.5
Infrastructure Security: Security Baselines: Application Hardening	4.3, 4.4, 4.5

LAB 4.1 DEFINING SECURITY TEMPLATES IN WINDOWS SERVER 2003

Objectives

One of the more difficult tasks for an administrator is determining the appropriate security settings for a network. There are so many possibilities that it is very easy to miss an important setting, often resulting in a network full of security holes. Microsoft has created security templates to assist administrators with this task. In addition to providing predefined templates, Microsoft also provides administrators with the ability to create custom templates. In this lab you will create a custom security template and manually adjust the security settings.

After completing this lab, you will be able to:

➤ Import Windows Server 2003 security templates

➤ Configure security settings for a custom template

➤ Secure the MACHINE hive of the Registry

➤ Configure Windows restricted groups

Materials Required

This lab requires the following:

➤ A Windows Server 2003 server with Administrator access

Estimated completion time: 20 minutes

ACTIVITY

1. Log on to your server as Administrator.

2. Click **Start**, click **Run**, type **mmc**, and then press **Enter**.

3. Click **File** on the menu bar, and then click **Add/Remove Snap-in**.

4. Click **Add**.

5. Scroll down and select **Security Templates**, as shown in Figure 4-1.

6. Click **Add**, and then click **Close**.

7. Click **OK**.

8. Expand **Security Templates**.

9. Expand **C:\WINDOWS\security\templates**, as shown in Figure 4-2.

10. Right-click **C:\WINDOWS\security\templates** and select **New Template**.

Figure 4-1 Selecting Security Templates

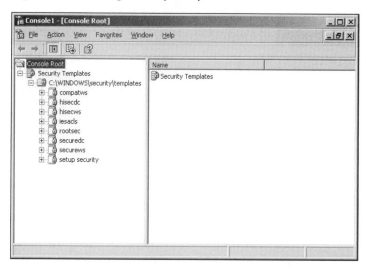

Figure 4-2 Expanding the security\templates folder

11. Enter **My Template** as the Template name, but leave the Description field blank.

12. Click **OK**.

13. Expand **My Template**, as shown in Figure 4-3.

14. Click **Restricted Groups**, and then right-click it.

15. Click **Add Group**.

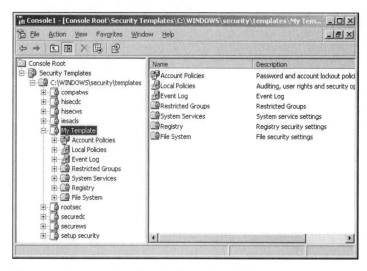

Figure 4-3 Expanding the My Template folder

16. Click **Browse**.

17. Type **Administrators** and then click **OK**.

18. Click **OK** twice.

19. Click **OK**.

20. Right-click **Registry**.

21. Select **Add Key**.

22. Select **MACHINE**.

23. Click **OK**.

24. Click **OK** to configure this key, and then propagate inheritable permissions to all subkeys, as shown in Figure 4-4.

25. Close the Console1 window. Click **Yes** to save the console.

26. Save the console with the name **My Console**.

27. Click **Yes** to save the security template.

28. Log off as Administrator.

Certification Objectives

Objectives for CompTIA Security+ Exam:

➤ Infrastructure Security: Security Baselines

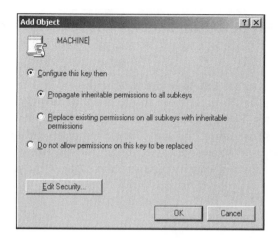

Figure 4-4 Propagating inheritable permissions to all subkeys

Review Questions

1. Which MMC snap-in is used to provide a centralized method of defining security?

    a. Computer Management

    b. Security Configuration and Analysis

    c. Security Templates

    d. Services

2. Security templates can be used to create security settings. True or False?

3. Which of the following is used in a security template to set security for user rights and logging for security events?

    a. Account Policies

    b. Local Policies

    c. Restricted Groups

    d. Registry

4. Which of the following is used to set security for local registry keys? (Choose all that apply.)

    a. regedit

    b. Local Policies section of a security template

    c. Registry section of a security template

    d. regedt32

5. The Local Group Policy is used to apply security templates, but these policies cannot be used to override a domain-based policy. True or False?

LAB 4.2 MANAGING WINDOWS SERVER 2003 SECURITY TEMPLATES

Objectives

On some occasions an administrator might not have the time or knowledge to secure a server manually with a custom template. As mentioned in the previous lab, Microsoft has created predefined security templates. These templates have three primary levels: basic, secure, and high secure. The issues surrounding the use of these templates are unknown. Because the administrator is relying on Microsoft to secure the server, the settings are difficult to track. In this lab you will apply a security template and evaluate the results.

After completing this lab, you will be able to:

➤ Apply a Windows Server 2003 security template

➤ Analyze the security configuration

Materials Required

This lab requires the following:

➤ Completion of Lab 4.1

➤ A Windows Server 2003 server with Administrator access

Estimated completion time: 15 minutes

ACTIVITY

1. Log on to your server as Administrator.

2. Click **Start**, click **All Programs**, click **Administrative Tools**, and select **My Console.msc**.

3. Click **File** on the menu bar, and then click **Add/Remove Snap-in**.

4. Click **Add**.

5. Select **Security Configuration and Analysis**.

6. Click **Add**, and then click **Close**.

7. Click **OK**.

8. Right-click **Security Configuration and Analysis**.

9. Click **Open Database**.

10. Enter **My Database.sdb** as the filename, and then click **Open**.

11. Select the **securedc.inf** template to import.

12. Click **Open**.

13. Right-click **Security Configuration and Analysis**.

14. Select **Configure Computer Now**.

15. Click **OK** to use My Database.log, as shown in Figure 4-5.

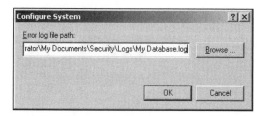

Figure 4-5 Selecting an error log file path

16. Right-click **Security Configuration and Analysis**.

17. Select **Analyze Computer Now**.

18. Click **OK** to use the My Database.log file.

19. Click **Security Configuration and Analysis** to select it, and then right-click it.

20. Select **View Log File** from the shortcut menu. You see a screen similar to the one shown in Figure 4-6.

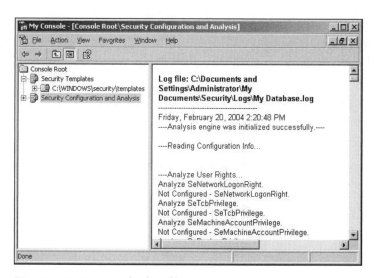

Figure 4-6 Viewing the log file

21. Explore the log file to see the security configuration.

22. Close all windows and log off as Administrator. If you are prompted to save the console or templates, click **No**.

Certification Objectives

Objectives for CompTIA Security+ Exam:

➤   Infrastructure Security: Security Baselines

Review Questions

1. Which of the following security templates can be used on a workstation? (Choose all that apply.)

    a. compatws

    b. hisecdc

    c. hisecws

    d. securews

2. Which of the following security templates is most likely to cause a problem with access to the server?

    a. basicdc

    b. hisecdc

    c. securedc

    d. the absence of a security template

3. The password policy set by the hisecdc template is identical to the securedc template. True or False?

4. Programs on a workstation that has been upgraded from Windows NT 4 to Windows Server 2003 fail to run as a member of the local user group. Which of the following security templates can be used?

    a. basicws

    b. compatsw

    c. compatws

    d. basicsw

5. What number of characters is the minimum password length requirement once the hisecdc template is applied?

    a. 0

    b. 7

    c. 8

    d. 14

LAB **4.3** PROTECTING THE SYSTEM ACCOUNTS DATABASE

Objectives

If intruders can gain physical access to a server, they can use utilities such as LOphtCrack to get a list of accounts and passwords. One way to prevent this intrusion is to encrypt the accounts database and assign a startup password. Beginning with Windows NT Service Pack 3, Microsoft provides the syskey tool to encrypt the accounts database. Syskey creates a random 128-bit encryption key, which is then protected with the system key. This program also offers the option to store the key on a floppy disk, which requires that the floppy disk be inserted to start the system. While this option makes a system very secure, it can also be dangerous; if the floppy disk is lost or corrupted, Windows must be reinstalled.

After completing this lab, you will be able to:

➤ Understand how to use the syskey command

➤ Configure a startup password

Materials Required

This lab requires the following:

➤ A Windows Server 2003 server with Administrator access

Estimated completion time: 10 minutes

ACTIVITY

If you plan to disable the encryption configured in this lab, be sure to create a Windows emergency repair disk (ERD) before proceeding.

NOTE

1. Log on to your server as Administrator.

2. Click **Start**, click **Run**, and type **syskey**. Press **Enter**.

3. Notice in Figure 4-7 that the **Encryption Disabled** option is not available. Windows Server 2003 encrypts the accounts database by default.

4. Click the **Update** button.

5. Click the **Password Startup** option, as shown in Figure 4-8.

6. Enter **password** as the password in the Password and Confirm text boxes.

7. Click **OK**. You are notified that the Account Database Startup Key was changed. Click **OK**.

Figure 4-7 Encryption options

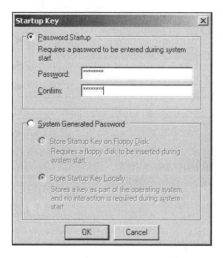

Figure 4-8 Selecting Password Startup

8. Restart the server. When the computer restarts, enter **password** in the Password text box, and then click **OK**.

9. Log on as Administrator, and then shut down the server.

Certification Objectives

Objectives for CompTIA Security+ Exam:

➤ Infrastructure Security: Devices

➤ Infrastructure Security: Security Baselines: Application Hardening

Review Questions

1. Which of the following is the file that contains the Windows accounts database?

    a. Accounts

    b. Secedit

    c. SAM

    d. SAM.dbf

2. If the system key is lost, it is impossible to recover the system. True or False?

3. Syskey encrypts which of the following registry hives? (Choose all that apply.)

    a. SOFTWARE

    b. SAM

    c. SYSTEM

    d. SECURITY

4. Which of the following are system security component files that are affected by syskey? (Choose all that apply.)

    a. Winlogon.exe

    b. SAM

    c. Samsrv.dll

    d. Samlib.dll

5. Which of the following methods are used by LOphtCrack to attack the accounts database? (Choose all that apply.)

    a. dictionary

    b. brute force

    c. random generated

    d. sniffing

LAB 4.4 CONFIGURING SERVICES AND PROCESSES

Objectives

When creating a bastion host, it is important to remove all unnecessary or unused services and programs. These services and programs can be used to exploit a weakness in the operating system or simply consume system resources. Programs such as Telnet, FTP, and any editors should be removed. Services for NetBIOS and the spooler should also be removed. The idea behind this procedure is to run only what is necessary and remove any programs that are not needed. This can be one of the more difficult steps in creating a bastion host,

4

because of the size of the operating systems. Windows Server 2003 has twice as many services available as Windows NT, making it even more difficult to harden.

After completing this lab, you will be able to:

➤ Configure services and processes

➤ Disable unnecessary services

Materials Required

This lab requires the following:

➤ Completion of Lab 4.3

➤ A Windows Server 2003 server with Administrator access

```
Estimated completion time: 20 minutes
```

LAB ACTIVITY

ACTIVITY

1. Boot to the server.

2. Enter **password** for the System Startup key, and then click **OK**.

3. Log on to the Windows Server 2003 server as Administrator.

4. Click **Start**, click **All Programs**, click **Administrative Tools**, and select **Services**.

5. Double-click the service for which you want to change settings. In the Properties dialog box, select the appropriate **Startup type**, and then click **OK**.

6. Configure the following Services to Start Automatically, if they are not already selected:
   - DNS Client
   - Event Log
   - Logical Disk Manager
   - Network Connections
   - Plug and Play
   - Protected Storage
   - Remote Procedure Call (RPC)
   - Secondary Logon
   - Security Accounts Manager
   - Windows Management Instrumentation
   - Windows Management Instrumentation Driver Extensions

7. If necessary, configure the **Logical Disk Manager Administrative Service** to start manually.

8. Disable the following services. (If you use DHCP, enable the DHCP client now.)
   - Automatic Updates
   - Smart Card
   - Task Scheduler

9. Close the Services window, and then log off as Administrator.

Certification Objectives

Objectives for CompTIA Security+ Exam:

➤ Infrastructure Security: Devices

➤ Infrastructure Security: Security Baselines: Application Hardening

Review Questions

1. Which of the following terms best describes a service that depends on another service to function properly?
   a. required
   b. dependence
   c. child
   d. parent

2. Which of the following is a valid startup type for services?
   a. manual
   b. automatic
   c. disabled
   d. all of the above

3. Services authenticate by using the user's account and password. True or False?

4. Which of the following is equivalent to stopping and starting a service?
   a. restart
   b. reset
   c. redo
   d. reboot

5. Which of the following services supports pass-through authentication for computers in a domain?

   a. Winlogon

   b. Workstation

   c. Net Logon

   d. Server

LAB **4.5** CONFIGURING NETWORK SETTINGS

Objectives

Once the operating system services and programs are hardened, you must restrict network access to the server. Most intrusion attempts take place over a network connection. These intrusions are not limited to remote users and hackers. The local network can also be used to exploit a weakness. During this lab, you will lock down TCP/IP and remove any unnecessary protocols.

After completing this lab, you will be able to:

➤ Configure advanced network settings

Materials Required

This lab requires the following:

➤ Completion of Lab 4.3

➤ A Windows Server 2003 server with Administrator access

Estimated completion time: 15 minutes

LAB ACTIVITY

ACTIVITY

1. Boot to the server you used in the previous lab.

2. Enter **password** as the system startup key in the Password text box, and then click **OK**.

3. Log on to the server as Administrator.

4. Click **Start**, right-click **My Computer**, and select **Properties**.

5. Click the **Hardware** tab, as shown in Figure 4-9.

6. Click the **Device Manager** button. You see a screen similar to the one shown in Figure 4-10.

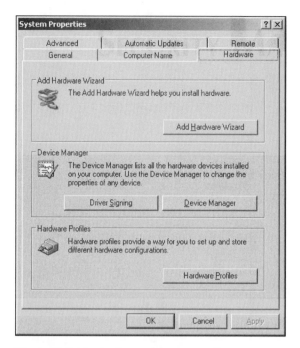

Figure 4-9 Hardware system properties

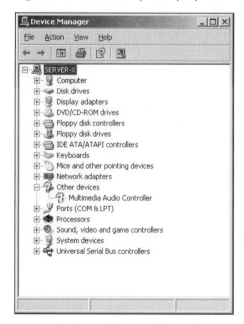

Figure 4-10 Device Manager window

7. Click **View** on the menu bar, and then click **Show hidden devices**.

8. Expand **Non-Plug and Play Drivers** if necessary, as shown in Figure 4-11.

Figure 4-11 Viewing Non-Plug and Play Drivers

9. Right-click **NetBios over Tcpip**, and select **Uninstall**.

10. Click **OK**, and then click **Yes** to restart the computer. Next, repeat Steps 2 and 3.

11. Click **Start**, click **All Programs**, click **Accessories**, click **Communications**, and then click **Network Connections**.

12. Right-click your **Local Area Connection**, and then select **Properties**.

13. Double-click **Internet Protocol (TCP/IP)**.

14. Click the **Advanced** button.

15. Click the **WINS** tab.

16. Click the **Disable NetBIOS over TCP/IP** option, as shown in Figure 4-12.

17. Click **OK** three times.

18. Repeat Steps 12 through 16 for all network cards.

19. NetBIOS is now disabled on this server. To test this, have the instructor disable DNS, if necessary, and ping another server in the room using only the computer name. The ping should fail.

20. Ping the same server using the IP address. The ping should work.

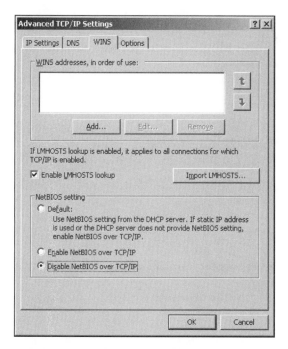

Figure 4-12 Disabling NetBIOS over TCP/IP

21. Close all windows and log off of the server.

Certification Objectives

Objectives for CompTIA Security+ Exam:

➤ Infrastructure Security: Devices

➤ Infrastructure Security: Security Baselines: Application Hardening

Review Questions

1. Which of the following is a broadcast-based protocol?

    a. TCP

    b. UDP

    c. NetBIOS

    d. IP

2. In Windows Server 2003, it is possible to filter which of the following protocols? (Choose all that apply.)

   a. TCP

   b. UDP

   c. NetBIOS

   d. IP

3. In Windows Server 2003, which of the following options can be used to filter? (Choose all that apply.)

   a. Permit All

   b. Deny All

   c. Permit Only

   d. Deny Only

4. Windows Server 2003 offers another level of TCP/IP protection by supporting which of the following?

   a. PGP

   b. IPSec

   c. EFS

   d. MD5

5. To configure TCP/IP filtering, you need to know which of the following? (Choose all that apply.)

   a. the protocol

   b. the port

   c. the IP address

   d. the network ID

CHAPTER FIVE

SECURING THE NETWORK INFRASTRUCTURE

Labs included in this chapter:

➤ Lab 5.1 Installing Snort on Windows-based Systems

➤ Lab 5.2 Capturing Packets with Snort

➤ Lab 5.3 Creating a Snort Rule Set

➤ Lab 5.4 Using IDScenter as a Front End for Snort

➤ Lab 5.5 Creating a Simple Honeypot

CompTIA Security+ Exam Objectives	
Objective	Lab
Infrastructure Security: Intrusion Detection	5.1, 5.3, 5.4
Infrastructure Security: Intrusion Detection: Network-based	5.2
Infrastructure Security: Intrusion Detection: Honeypots	5.5

LAB 5.1 INSTALLING SNORT ON WINDOWS-BASED SYSTEMS

Objectives

Being able to recover from a security breach is a vital part of network security. However, this is a reactive way to secure your network, and it might contribute to considerable downtime. A proactive approach is to put systems in place to keep intrusions from occurring, or to have a plan for preventing intrusions from doing damage if they do infiltrate your network. The primary proactive tool for network security is an intrusion detection system (IDS). An IDS functions by listening to the network for recognized attacks, and then reporting the findings to a network administrator. An IDS is excellent for detecting and reporting problems, but not for repairing damage. It is still necessary for a network administrator to properly repair the damage done by a security breach. An example of an IDS is an open-source solution named Snort.

After completing this lab, you will be able to:

➤ Install WinPcap, a packet capture utility

➤ Install Snort for Windows

Materials Required

This lab requires the following:

➤ Two Windows Server 2003 servers with Administrator access

➤ Snort 2.1.2 (You can download it from *www.snort.org/dl/binaries/win32*)

➤ WinPcap (You can download it from *www.snort.org/dl/contrib/other_stuff*)

Note that you can also use *www.snort.org* to help answer some of the review questions in the Chapter 5 labs, if necessary. Note also that the Web addresses listed in this chapter were correct at the time of publication, but that Web addresses sometimes change over time.

> Estimated completion time: 15 minutes

ACTIVITY

The servers used in this activity are called Server-X and Server-Y. Please substitute the names of your own servers.

1. Log on to Server-X as Administrator.

2. Create the folder **snort** on your local hard drive (C:\).

3. Copy **WinPcap_2_3.exe** to the snort folder.

4. Double-click the **WinPcap_2_3.exe** file in the snort folder.

5. Click **Next**, accept the license agreement, and then click **Next** two times. You receive a message that WinPcap is installed.

6. Click **OK**.

7. Restart Server-X and log on as Administrator.

8. Double-click the **Snort-2_1_2.exe** file to start the installation. Accept the default settings.

9. Repeat Steps 1 through 8 on Server-Y.

10. Log off Server-X and Server-Y.

Certification Objectives

Objectives for CompTIA Security+ Exam:

➤ Infrastructure Security: Intrusion Detection

Review Questions

1. An IDS evaluates a suspected intrusion once it has taken place and signals an alarm. True or False?

2. Which of the following IDSs logs the information and signals an alert?
   a. network-based
   b. host-based
   c. passive
   d. reactive

3. Which of the following IDSs responds to suspicious activity by logging off a user or by reprogramming the firewall to block network traffic from the suspected malicious source?
   a. network-based
   b. host-based
   c. passive
   d. reactive

4. Which of the following IDS methods analyze information and compare it to the contents of large databases of attack signatures? (Choose all that apply.)
   a. anomaly
   b. misuse
   c. passive
   d. reactive

5. A firewall limits the access between networks to prevent intrusion, and does not signal an attack from inside the network. True or False?

LAB 5.2 CAPTURING PACKETS WITH SNORT

Objectives

The first requirement of a network-based IDS is to act as a sniffer on the network. Because the source of the attack is unknown, the IDS must be able to listen to anything that travels across the network. A network-based IDS looks for attack signatures that usually indicate malicious intent. Another type of IDS is host-based, which checks for signatures in log files. This type of IDS does not sniff the network, but it might examine the Windows Event logs. In this lab you will use Snort as a packet sniffer to capture ICMP packets from a ping and create log files.

After completing this lab, you will be able to:

➤ Understand how to use Snort to capture data packets

➤ View the contents of the data packets

➤ Create log files

Materials Required

This lab requires the following:

➤ Two Windows Server 2003 servers with Snort and WinPcap installed

➤ Administrator access to the servers

➤ A crossover cable

Estimated completion time: 30 minutes

ACTIVITY

LAB ACTIVITY

The servers used in this activity are called Server-X and Server-Y. Please substitute the names of your own servers.

1. Unplug the network connection to the classroom network. Make sure that Server-X and Server-Y are connected with a crossover cable, and that they are not connected to a network.

2. Disable the classroom NICs. This step ensures that the servers are isolated.

3. Log on to Server-X as Administrator.

4. Click **Start**, click **All Programs**, click **Accessories**, and then click **Command Prompt**.

5. Type **cd\snort\bin**, and then press **Enter**.

6. Type **snort −v**, and then press **Enter**. You see a screen similar to the one shown in Figure 5-1.

Figure 5-1   Initializing Snort

7. Log on to Server-Y as Administrator.

8. Click **Start**, click **All Programs**, click **Accessories**, and then click **Command Prompt**.

9. Type **ping Server-X** and press **Enter**.

10. On Server-X, press **Ctrl+C** to view the results, as shown in Figure 5-2. Notice the ECHO and ECHO REPLY.

11. Scroll down the command window to view the statistics, as shown in Figure 5-3. Notice that ICMP was the protocol used.

12. On Server-X, type **snort −v −d** at the command line to view the packet data.

13. Press **Enter**.

14. On Server-Y, type **ping Server-X** and press **Enter**.

15. On Server-X, press **Ctrl+C** to view the results. You see a screen similar to the one shown in Figure 5-4.

16. Type **snort −dev −l \snort\log** at the command line and press **Enter**.

17. Ping Server-X from Server-Y.

18. On Server-X, press **Ctrl+C**.

19. Navigate to the C:\snort\log folder and examine the contents. Use Notepad to open the files.

20. Repeat Steps 3 through 19 on Server-Y. (The purpose of this step is to reverse roles; when you repeat the steps, treat all references to Server-X as Server-Y, and vice versa.)

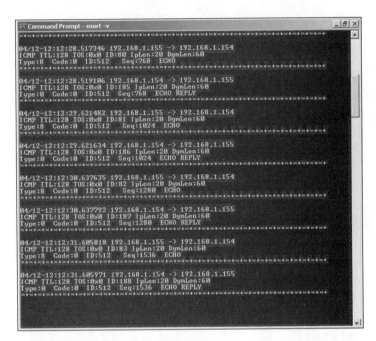

Figure 5-2   A Snort ping capture

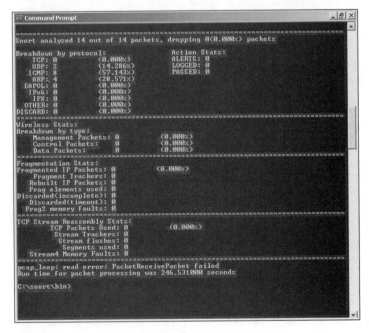

Figure 5-3   Snort ping capture statistics

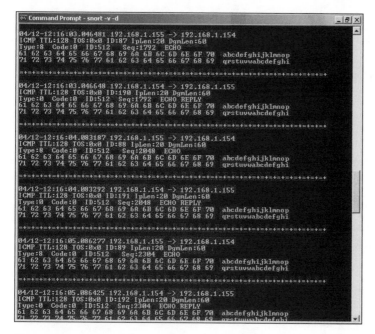

Figure 5-4   A Snort ping capture with data

21. Close all windows and log off Server-X and Server-Y. Remove the crossover cable, reconnect the computers to the network, and restart Server-X and Server-Y.

Certification Objectives

Objectives for CompTIA Security+ Exam:

➤ Infrastructure Security: Intrusion Detection: Network-based

Review Questions

1. Which IDS method is operating system-dependent?
   a. host-based
   b. log-based
   c. network-based
   d. event-based

2. Which of the following is a technique for recognizing an attack signature?
   a. frequency
   b. pattern
   c. correlation

d. statistical

e. all of the above

3. Which method of IDS is best suited for detecting Trojan horses such as BackOrifice?

a. host-based

b. log-based

c. network-based

d. event-based

4. Which method of IDS is capable of real-time detection?

a. host-based

b. log-based

c. network-based

d. event-based

5. Which method of IDS is best suited for encrypted and switched environments?

a. host-based

b. log-based

c. network-based

d. event-based

LAB 5.3 CREATING A SNORT RULE SET

Objectives

While an IDS can be very useful in detecting intrusions, it can also produce more information than necessary in the log files. If the log files are too large to manage, they are not useful. An IDS can sniff all traffic, but the ability to create rules allows a network engineer to filter just the necessary signatures. For example, if you are monitoring a network that contains a Web server, it doesn't make sense to log requests on port 80. But you might want to log Telnet and other protocols for attempts on the network to see if someone is trying to exploit a weakness. In this lab you will create a simple Snort rule set to alert you when the ICMP protocol is used.

After completing this lab, you will be able to:

➤ Create a Snort rule set

➤ Test the rule set on the network

Materials Required

This lab requires the following:

➤ Two Windows Server 2003 servers with Snort installed

➤ Administrator access to the servers

Estimated completion time: 15–20 minutes

ACTIVITY

The servers used in this activity are called Server-X and Server-Y. Please substitute the names of your own servers.

1. Log on to Server-X as Administrator.

2. Click **Start**, click **Run**, and type **notepad**.

3. Click **OK**.

4. Enter the information shown in Figure 5-5.

Figure 5-5   A Snort rule set

5. Save the file as **c:\snort\rules\new.rules**. Close Notepad. Navigate to the file you just created, and rename it to remove the .txt extension.

6. On Server-X, click **Start**, click **Run**, and then type **cmd**. Click **OK**.

7. Type **cd\snort\bin** at the command line, and then press **Enter**.

8. Type **snort –c \snort\rules\new.rules –l \snort\log** at the command line, and then press **Enter**.

9. From Server-Y, open Internet Explorer and enter **\\Server-X** in the Address field. Press **Enter**.

10. On Server-X, press **Ctrl+C**.

11. Navigate to the **C:\snort\log** folder, and open the subfolder with the appropriate IP address in the name.

12. Examine the Web traffic logged in the **TCP_*-80.ids** file, where * represents a four-digit number. It should look similar to the file shown in Figure 5-6.

Figure 5-6   A Snort log file containing Web traffic

13. On Server-X, type **snort –c \snort\rules\new.rules –l \snort\log**, and then press **Enter**.

14. On Server-Y, click **Start**, click **All Programs**, click **Accessories**, and then click **Command Prompt**. Type **ping Server-X** and press **Enter**.

15. On Server-X, press **Ctrl+C**.

16. Navigate to the **C:\snort\log** folder.

17. Examine the contents of the **alert.ids** file. It should look similar to the file shown in Figure 5-7.

18. Repeat Steps 1 through 17 on Server-Y. (The purpose of this step is to reverse roles; when you repeat the steps, treat all references to Server-X as Server-Y, and vice versa.)

19. Close all windows and log off Server-X and Server-Y.

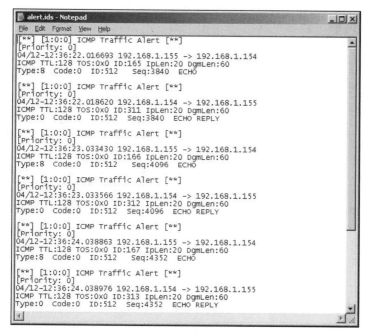

Figure 5-7   A Snort ICMP traffic alert log

Certification Objectives

Objectives for CompTIA Security+ Exam:

➤ Infrastructure Security: Intrusion Detection

Review Questions

1. Which of the following is equivalent to all IP addresses when creating Snort rules?

   a. all

   b. any

   c. 0.0.0.0

   d. 255.255.255.255

2. Which of the following commands logs TCP traffic from any port going to ports less than or equal to 6000 on the 192.168.1.0 network?

   a. log tcp any any -> 192.168.1.0/24 :6000

   b. log tcp any any -> 192.168.1.0/24 <=6000

   c. log udp any any -> 192.168.1.0/24 :6000

   d. log tcp any any -> 192.168.1.0/24 any

3. Which of the following protocols can Snort analyze?

    a. TCP

    b. UDP

    c. ICMP

    d. IP

    e. all of the above

4. Which of the following operators is used to log port ranges?

    a. >

    b. <

    c. :

    d. ;

5. Which of the following Snort keywords prints a message in alerts and packet logs?

    a. print

    b. msg

    c. type

    d. alert

LAB 5.4 USING IDSCENTER AS A FRONT END FOR SNORT

Objectives

An IDS can be very helpful in protecting a network from intrusions, but the programs themselves are not always easy to use, as you might have noticed in the previous labs with Snort. This problem is not uncommon in the security field. One way to fix the problem is to use a front-end program that does the difficult work for you. In this lab you will use IDScenter to make Snort easier to use, and to offer some additional features that are not available with the command-line application.

After completing this lab, you will be able to:

➤   Install the IDScenter front end for Snort

➤   Configure and run IDScenter

Materials Required

This lab requires the following:

➤ Two Windows Server 2003 servers with Snort installed

➤ IDScenter (You can download it from *www.snort.org/dl/contrib/front_ends/ids_center*; click the idscenter.zip link)

➤ Administrator access to the servers

5

Estimated completion time: 45 minutes

LAB ACTIVITY

ACTIVITY

The servers used in this activity are called Server-X and Server-Y. Please substitute the names of your own servers.

1. Log on to Server-X as Administrator.

2. Run the **setup.exe** file from the idscenter.zip file.

3. The installation wizard begins. Click **Next**.

4. Click **Next** to accept the default installation location of **C:\Program Files\IDScenter**.

5. Click **Next** to select the Program Group **Snort IDScenter**.

6. Click **Install**.

7. Uncheck the **View info.txt** check box.

8. Click **Finish**.

9. Double-click the **IDScenter** icon on the desktop. The program loads and puts an icon in the system tray.

10. Double-click the icon in the system tray.

11. In the Snort setup section, choose the location of the snort.exe file, as shown in Figure 5-8.

12. Enter *Server-X IP address/32* in the Home network field, as shown in Figure 5-9. (Replace *Server-X IP address* with the actual IP address.)

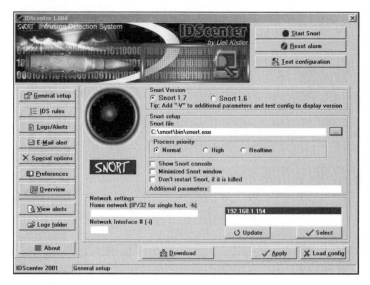

Figure 5-8   IDScenter opening screen

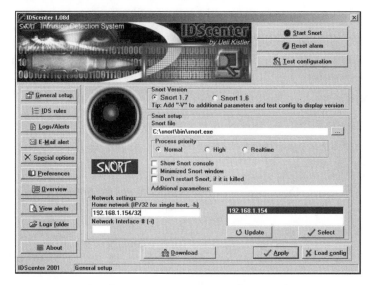

Figure 5-9   Configuring Snort setup and network settings

13. Click the **IDS rules** button.

14. Choose the **new.rules** file you created in the previous lab exercise as the Snort IDS rule set, as shown in Figure 5-10.

15. Click the **Logs/Alerts** button.

16. Enter **C:\snort\log** in the Set directory for Snort logfiles field.

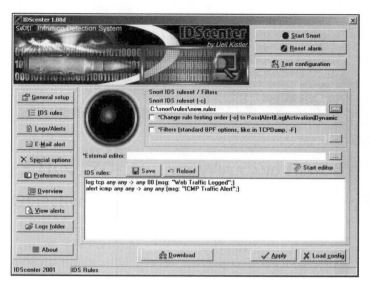

Figure 5-10   Loading IDS rules

17. Check the **Set alert mode (-A)** option.

18. Check the **Dump the raw packets (-X)** option, as shown in Figure 5-11.

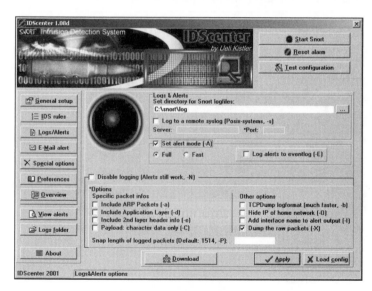

Figure 5-11   Configuring logs and alerts

19. Click the **Special options** button.

20. Check the ***Start this program when receiving an alert** option.

21. Enter **net send** *Server-X IP address* **Alert, Check the Snort Logs!,** as shown in Figure 5-12. (Replace *Server-X IP address* with the actual IP address.)

Figure 5-12 Running an external program to send an administrative alert

22. Click the **Overview** button, and then click **Apply**. Notice the Snort command line shown in Figure 5-13.

Figure 5-13 IDScenter Snort configuration overview

23. Click **Start Snort**.

24. Start the Messenger service on Server-X and Server-Y. Ping Server-X from Server-Y. You receive a message similar to the one shown in Figure 5-14.

Figure 5-14   An IDScenter alert message

25. Click **OK** to close each message window that appears.

26. Click the **View alerts** button to view the details, and then close the Alert.ids window.

27. Click **Stop Snort**.

28. Repeat Steps 1 through 27 on Server-Y. (The purpose of this step is to reverse roles; when you repeat the steps, treat all references to Server-X as Server-Y, and vice versa.)

29. Close all windows and log off Server-X and Server-Y.

Certification Objectives

Objectives for CompTIA Security+ Exam:

➤ Infrastructure Security: Intrusion Detection

Review Questions

1. IDScenter can alert an administrator with which of the following?

   a. e-mail

   b. sound

   c. visual alerts

   d. all of the above

2. The Snort command-line application offers a testing feature that is not available in IDScenter. True or False?

3. IDScenter can create log files in which of the following formats? (Choose all that apply.)

    a. text

    b. HTML

    c. PDF

    d. XML

    e. all of the above

4. IDScenter can execute a program when an attack is detected. True or False?

5. If you want to be informed about all attacks coming from a WAN, you should deploy the IDS _____ .

    a. in front of a firewall

    b. behind a firewall

    c. on a firewall

    d. in place of a firewall

LAB 5.5 CREATING A SIMPLE HONEYPOT

Objectives

Honeypots are systems that are designed to be probed, attacked, and even compromised to help reduce risk in an organization. There are two types of honeypots: production, which is used to protect a network by acting as a decoy system, and research, which is used to gain information on the hacker community and to test the strength of your network security. While honeypots might not be good for prevention, they can be an excellent point of detection. Because of their simple design, they are also easy to configure. In this lab you will install, configure, and test a simple honeypot program, BackOfficer.

After completing this lab, you will be able to:

➤ Install and configure BackOfficer

➤ Detect a Telnet attempt

Materials Required

This lab requires the following:

➤ Two Windows Server 2003 servers with all of the latest service packs and hot fixes installed

➤ BackOfficer (You can download it from *www.nfr.com/resource/backOfficer.php*; the download is a .tar file, which is a UNIX format, but you can open the file with WinZip and extract the Windows version. If you have trouble downloading the Windows version, ask your instructor for help.)

➤ Administrator access to the servers

Estimated completion time: 20–25 minutes

LAB ACTIVITY

ACTIVITY

The servers used in this activity are called Server-X and Server-Y. Please substitute the names of your own servers.

1. Log on to Server-X as Administrator.

2. Double-click the **nfrbofl.exe** file (or the current executable filename).

3. Click **OK** to accept the default installation location of **C:\Program Files\ NFR\BackOfficer Friendly**. You receive the message shown in Figure 5-15.

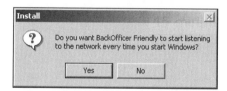

Figure 5-15 BackOfficer option to start concurrently with Windows

4. Click **Yes**. You receive a second message, shown in Figure 5-16.

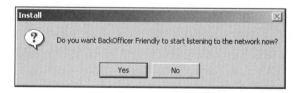

Figure 5-16 Option to start BackOfficer now

5. Click **Yes**.

6. Click **OK** to finish. Notice the new icon in the system tray.

7. Right-click the **BackOfficer** icon in the system tray, and then click **Details**.

8. Click **Options**.

9. Select **Listen for Telnet**.

10. On Server-Y, click **Start**, click **All Programs**, click **Accessories**, and then click **Command Prompt**. Type **telnet Server-X** and press **Enter**. Notice the Telnet detection on Server-X, as shown in Figure 5-17.

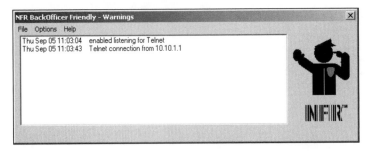

Figure 5-17   BackOfficer Telnet detection

11. Click **Options** on the menu bar and select **Listen for HTTP**. If IIS is installed, you receive the message shown in Figure 5-18.

Figure 5-18   BackOfficer error message

 The purpose of the honeypot is to keep an eye on potential attacks, as well as provide a potential hacker with a fake target. If you want to listen for HTTP, disable the IIS service.

NOTE

12. Repeat Steps 1 through 11 on Server-Y. (The purpose of this step is to reverse roles; when you repeat the steps, treat all references to Server-X as Server-Y, and vice versa.)

13. Close all windows and log off Server-X and Server-Y.

Certification Objectives

Objectives for CompTIA Security+ Exam:

➤ Infrastructure Security: Intrusion Detection: Honeypots

Review Questions

1. A honeypot contains no critical data or applications, but has enough interesting data to lure a hacker. True or False?

2. Honeypots are most successful on which of the following servers? (Choose all that apply.)

   a. file

   b. print

   c. Web

   d. DNS

3. Which of the following is another term used to describe a honeypot?

   a. sacrificial lamb

   b. decoy

   c. booby trap

   d. all of the above

4. Which of the following functions can a honeypot provide? (Choose all that apply.)

   a. prevention

   b. detection

   c. reaction

   d. correction

   e. all of the above

5. The most commonly used honeypot is a research honeypot. True or False?

5

PROTECTING BASIC COMMUNICATIONS

Labs included in this chapter:

➤ Lab 6.1 Configuring Internet Explorer Security

➤ Lab 6.2 Configuring Internet Explorer Privacy

➤ Lab 6.3 Configuring Internet Explorer Content Filtering

➤ Lab 6.4 Configuring Internet Explorer Advanced Security Settings

➤ Lab 6.5 Manually Blocking Web Sites and Pop-ups

CompTIA Security+ Exam Objectives	
Objective	Lab
Communication Security: Web: HTTP/S	6.1
Communication Security: Web: Vulnerabilities: Cookies	6.2
Communication Security: Web	6.3, 6.4, 6.5

LAB 6.1 CONFIGURING INTERNET EXPLORER SECURITY

Objectives

Most large companies have advanced firewalls and proxy services that allow them to filter or block certain content from employee desktops. This is a necessary feature, but it is not always practical, especially for small to mid-sized companies. Fortunately, Microsoft has built-in security features that are available to users of Internet Explorer. In this lab, you block the downloading of files by configuring Microsoft Internet Explorer to use the default settings for restricted sites.

After completing this lab, you will be able to:

➤ Configure trusted sites in Microsoft Internet Explorer 6

➤ Configure restricted sites to block file downloads in Internet Explorer 6

Materials Required

This lab requires the following:

➤ A Windows Server 2003 server with Internet Explorer 6 installed

➤ Administrator access to the server

Estimated completion time: 20–25 minutes

ACTIVITY

1. Log on as Administrator.

2. Open **Internet Explorer**. Click **Tools** on the menu bar, and then click **Internet Options**.

3. You might receive a notification that Internet Explorer's Enhanced Security Configuration is enabled. Check the box labeled **In the future, do not show this message**, and then click **OK**.

4. Click the **Security** tab. You see the window shown in Figure 6-1.

5. Click the **Trusted sites** icon.

6. Click the **Sites** button.

7. Uncheck the **Require server verification (https:) for all sites in this zone** option, if it is checked.

8. Add the **www.course.com** Web site to the zone by typing the URL in the top text box, and then click **Add**, as shown in Figure 6-2.

9. Click **Close**.

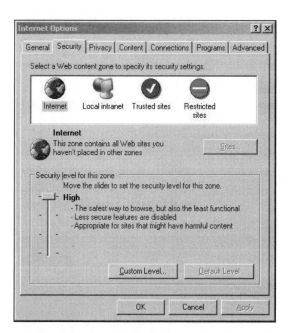

Figure 6-1   Internet security options

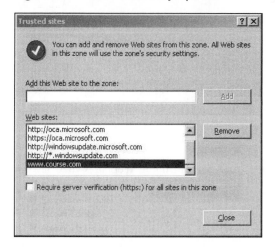

Figure 6-2   Adding a trusted Web site

10. Click the **Restricted sites** icon.

11. Click the **Sites** button.

12. Add **www.kazaa.com** and **ftp.microsoft.com** to the zone, as explained in Step 8.

13. Click **Close**.

14. Click **OK** to close the Internet Options dialog box.

15. Enter **www.kazaa.com** in the Internet Explorer Address text box, and then press **Enter**. If you see a notification message, click **Close** until you return to Internet Explorer. Kazaa fails to load.

16. Enter **ftp.microsoft.com** and press **Enter**. You should receive a message similar to the one shown in Figure 6-3.

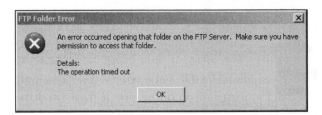

Figure 6-3   Error message that appears when Web site fails to load

Because URLs can be redirected, this activity does not reflect the best way to block file downloads. However, this activity can provide a helpful "quick fix."

TIP

17. Close all windows and log off.

Certification Objectives

Objectives for CompTIA Security+ Exam:

➤ Communication Security: Web: HTTP/S

Review Questions

1. Which of the following is a zone containing all Web sites that have not been placed in other zones?

   a. Internet

   b. local intranet

   c. trusted sites

   d. restricted sites

2. Which of the following is a zone containing Web sites that could damage your system?

   a. Internet

   b. local intranet

   c. trusted sites

   d. restricted sites

3. Which of the following is a zone containing Web sites that you believe will not damage your system?

   a. Internet

   b. local intranet

   c. trusted sites

   d. restricted sites

4. Which of the following Custom Level security settings requires a user-name and password for user authentication?

   a. high

   b. medium

   c. medium-low

   d. low

   e. none of the above

5. Which of the following Custom Level security settings allows for anonymous user authentication?

   a. high

   b. medium

   c. medium-low

   d. low

   e. none of the above

LAB 6.2 CONFIGURING INTERNET EXPLORER PRIVACY

Objectives

One issue many users have with Web browsing is that anyone on the Internet can write information to a user's computer hard drive. One example of this ability is the use of cookies. Cookies can be valuable to both the user and the company that deposits them. For example, if you go to an e-commerce site and fill out a form with all of your important data, a cookie is often placed on your computer by the e-commerce site to help remember you when you visit again. This way, you do not have to enter the same data every time you visit the site. However, this capability can also be a major security risk. Using the cookie on your computer, anyone with access to your computer could go to the e-commerce site and purchase goods in your name without your knowledge. In this lab, you will configure Internet Explorer's Privacy settings to block the use of cookies.

After completing this lab, you will be able to:

➤ Configure Internet Explorer 6 Privacy settings

➤ Understand the different settings for cookies in Internet Explorer 6

Materials Required

This lab requires the following:

➤ A Windows Server 2003 server with Internet Explorer 6 installed

➤ Administrator access to the server

Estimated completion time: 15 minutes

ACTIVITY

1. Log on as Administrator.

2. Open **Internet Explorer**. Click **Tools** on the menu bar, and then click **Internet Options**.

3. Click the **Privacy** tab.

4. Slide the **Settings** bar to **High**, as shown in Figure 6-4. This blocks all cookies that do not comply with the W3C P3P.

TIP   The Platform for Privacy Preferences Project (P3P), developed by the World Wide Web Consortium (W3C), is emerging as an industry standard that provides a simple, automated way for users to gain more control over the use of personal information on Web sites they visit.

5. Click the **Edit** button to add Web sites that you want to allow to bypass the settings.

6. Type **www.yahoo.com** in the **Address of Web site** text box.

7. Click **Allow**. Notice that only the domain is added to the Managed Web sites list, as shown in Figure 6-5.

8. Click **OK**.

9. Click **OK**.

10. Enter **www.msn.com** in the Internet Explorer Address text box, and then press **Enter**.

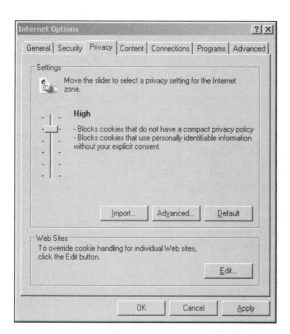

Figure 6-4   Internet privacy options

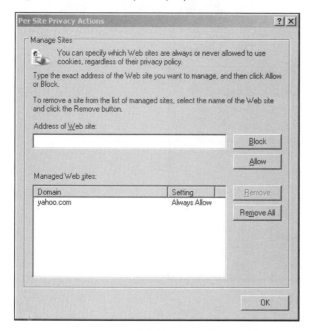

Figure 6-5   Managing privacy options for Web sites

11. You receive the Internet Explorer Enhanced Security Configuration message, as shown in Figure 6-6. You can view a report similar to the one shown in Figure 6-7 if you double-click the Privacy Report icon at the bottom of the browser.

12. Click **Close** as many times as necessary to dismiss the message shown in Figure 6-6.

Figure 6-6   Message that Web site access is blocked

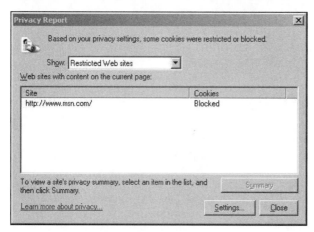

Figure 6-7   Web privacy report

13. Enter **www.yahoo.com** in the Internet Explorer Address text box, and then press **Enter**. Notice that the privacy warning is absent.

14. To reset the privacy settings, return to the Internet Options dialog box, click the **Privacy** tab, and click the **Default** button. The settings return to Medium, the default setting in Internet Explorer.

15. Click **OK**, close all windows, and log off.

Certification Objectives

Objectives for CompTIA Security+ Exam:

➤ Communication Security: Web: Vulnerabilities: Cookies

Review Questions

1. A cookie is a small text file that stores information a server can use. True or False?

2. Which of the following privacy settings block all cookies without a Compact Privacy Policy? (Choose all that apply.)
   a. block all cookies
   b. high
   c. medium–high
   d. medium
   e. low
   f. accept all cookies

3. Which of the following privacy settings does not restrict first-party cookies? (Choose all that apply.)
   a. block all cookies
   b. high
   c. medium–high
   d. medium
   e. low
   f. accept all cookies

4. Which of the following privacy settings is likely to cause some Web pages to fail to load? (Choose all that apply.)
   a. block all cookies
   b. high
   c. medium–high
   d. medium
   e. low
   f. accept all cookies

5. Which of the following privacy settings is the default policy setting?
   a. block all cookies
   b. high

    c. medium–high

    d. medium

    e. low

    f. accept all cookies

LAB 6.3 CONFIGURING INTERNET EXPLORER CONTENT FILTERING

Objectives

Recall that large companies can filter content by using a proxy server. Internet Explorer can also filter content based on RSACi settings. The Recreational Software Advisory Council (RSAC), which became the Internet Content Rating Association (ICRA), is an independent organization that works to protect children from potentially harmful material on the Internet. RSACi is their content rating system for Internet sites. The categories you can filter are Language, Nudity, Sex, and Violence. You can individually configure each of these categories to meet your needs.

After completing this lab, you will be able to:

➤ Configure content filtering in Internet Explorer 6

➤ Password-protect the content filtering settings

Materials Required

This lab requires the following:

➤ A Windows Server 2003 server with Internet Explorer 6 installed

➤ Administrator access to the server

> Estimated completion time: 15–20 minutes

LAB ACTIVITY

ACTIVITY

1. Log on as Administrator.

2. Open **Internet Explorer**. Click **Tools** on the menu bar, and then click **Internet Options**.

3. Click the **Content** tab. You see a screen similar to the one shown in Figure 6-8.

4. In the Content Advisor section, click **Enable**.

5. The Content Advisor window appears, as shown in Figure 6-9.

Figure 6-8   Internet content options

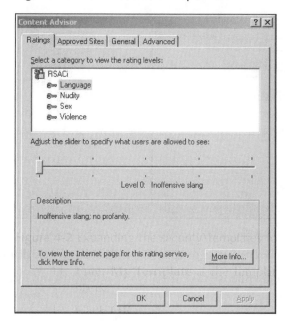

Figure 6-9   Internet Content Advisor

6. Leave all of the settings at **Level 0**; this is the most restrictive setting. You might want to slide the bars for each of the categories to see what each level allows.

7. Click the **General** tab of the Content Advisor window. The window shown in Figure 6-10 appears.

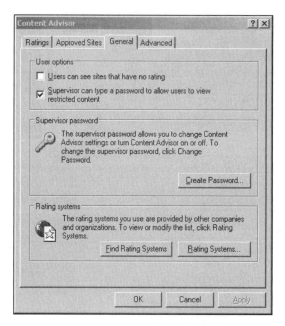

Figure 6-10 General Content Advisor settings

8. Click the **Create Password** button. The window shown in Figure 6-11 appears.

9. Enter **password** in the Password and Confirm password text boxes.

10. Enter **Course** in the Hint text box, and then click **OK**. You receive a message that the supervisor password was successfully created.

11. Click **OK**, and then click **OK** again to close the Content Advisor.

12. Click **OK**, and then click **OK** again to close the Internet Options dialog box.

13. Enter **www.nick.com** (a children's site from Nickelodeon) in the Internet Explorer Address text box, and then press **Enter**. You receive the message shown in Figure 6-12.

14. Enter **password** in the Password text box, and then click **OK**. You are granted access to the site.

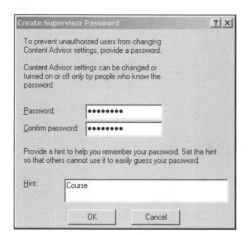

Figure 6-11   Creating a password in Content Advisor

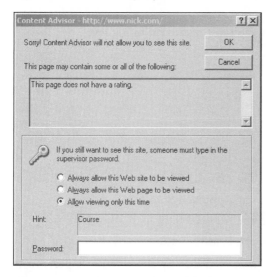

Figure 6-12   Content Advisor blocking access to a Web site

These settings are very restrictive, and you might be prompted multiple times per site.

TIP

15. Return to the **Content** tab of the Internet Options dialog box and click **Disable**.

16. When prompted to enter the password, enter **password** and click **OK**. You receive the message shown in Figure 6-13.

17. Click **OK**, and then click **OK** again to close the Internet Options dialog box.

Figure 6-13   Notification that Content Advisor is off

18. Close Internet Explorer and log off.

Certification Objectives

Objectives for CompTIA Security+ Exam:

➤   Communication Security: Web

Review Questions

1. Which of the following is the most restrictive rating level?

   a. Level 0

   b. Level 1

   c. Level 2

   d. Level 3

   e. Level 4

2. A way to bypass the Ratings settings is to _____ .

   a. allow the Web site in the Advanced settings

   b. allow the Web site in the Approved Sites list

   c. allow the Web site in the Allowed Sites list

   d. You cannot override the Ratings settings.

3. The supervisor can access restricted sites by entering the supervisor password. True or False?

4. What is the default response by the Content Advisor if the Web site does not have a rating?

   a. The user can view the page.

   b. The user cannot view the page.

   c. The user can view the page by manually entering a rating.

   d. none of the above

5. You just configured the Content Advisor settings; all but one of the computers on the network appear to bypass the rules. What could be the problem?

   a. The rules were configured incorrectly.

   b. You forgot to apply the rules.

   c. The site that was allowed was not rated.

   d. The temporary Internet files have not been deleted.

6

LAB **6.4** CONFIGURING INTERNET EXPLORER ADVANCED SECURITY SETTINGS

Objectives

In addition to cookies, Internet Explorer can store information about your Web browsing habits by caching. This can be a major problem in areas that require high-level security. Most users are aware of temporary Internet files and how to remove them. Temporary Internet files are used as a local cache to increase the speed of Web browsing, but the files can also track your path on the Web. User-names and passwords can be stored to save you time, but they might also allow unauthorized access to resources. Fortunately, you can resolve these issues by using the Advanced Security settings in Internet Explorer.

After completing this lab, you will be able to:

➤ Configure the advanced settings in Internet Explorer 6

➤ Protect your information related to Web browsing

Materials Required

This lab requires the following:

➤ A Windows Server 2003 server with Internet Explorer 6 installed

➤ Administrator access to the server

Estimated completion time: 10 minutes

LAB ACTIVITY

ACTIVITY

1. Log on as Administrator.

2. Open **Internet Explorer**. Click **Tools** on the menu bar, and then click **Internet Options**.

3. Click the **Advanced** tab.

4. Scroll down to the **Security** settings, as shown in Figure 6-14.

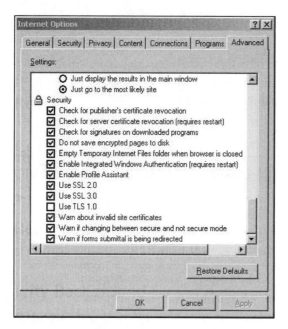

Figure 6-14   Advanced Internet options

5. Verify that the **Empty Temporary Internet Files folder when browser is closed** option is checked.

6. Click the **Content** tab.

7. Click the **AutoComplete** button.

8. In the "Use AutoComplete for" section, uncheck the box next to **User names and passwords on forms**, as shown in Figure 6-15.

9. Click **OK** to close the AutoComplete Settings window.

10. Click **OK** to close the Internet Options dialog box.

11. Close all remaining windows and log off.

Certification Objectives

Objectives for CompTIA Security+ Exam:

➤   Communication Security: Web

Figure 6-15 AutoComplete settings

Review Questions

1. If you want to prevent secure files from being stored in temporary Internet files, you can check which of the following Security options?

   a. Do not save encrypted file to disk

   b. Empty Temporary Internet Files folder when browser is closed

   c. Use Fortezza

   d. Do not save Certificates to disk

2. When you enable the option "Empty Temporary Internet Files folder when browser is closed," it also deletes all cookies. True or False?

3. All secure Web sites support which of the following protocols?

   a. SSL 2.0

   b. SSL 3.0

   c. TLS 1.0

   d. PCT 1.0

4. Which of the following protocols was developed by Microsoft?

   a. SSL 2.0

   b. SSL 3.0

   c. TLS 1.0

   d. PCT 1.0

5. Which of the following protocols requires a Crypto Card?

   a. EFS

   b. Fortezza

   c. Crypto

   d. TLS 1.0

LAB 6.5 MANUALLY BLOCKING WEB SITES AND POP-UPS

Objectives

One of the most useful yet annoying features of Web browsing is the "pop-up." Pop-ups can be an effective form of advertising, but they can annoy the user when accessing Web sites. A few commercial and freeware products can block pop-ups, although none of them works 100% of the time. Another quick and easy method is to redirect the Web site to the local loopback. This method uses the local hosts file to disable pop-ups and block access to Web sites.

After completing this lab, you will be able to:

➤ Edit the hosts file to redirect Web sites and prevent access to those sites

➤ Edit the hosts file to stop pop-up ads

Materials Required

This lab requires the following:

➤ A Windows Server 2003 server with Internet Explorer 6 installed

➤ Administrator access to the server

Estimated completion time: 20 minutes

ACTIVITY

1. Log on as Administrator.

2. Click the **Start** button, and then click **Search**.

3. Type **hosts** in the top text box, and then click **Search**. The results should be similar to the screen shown in Figure 6-16.

4. Right-click the **hosts** file located in **%systemroot%\system32\drivers\etc**.

5. Select **Open**.

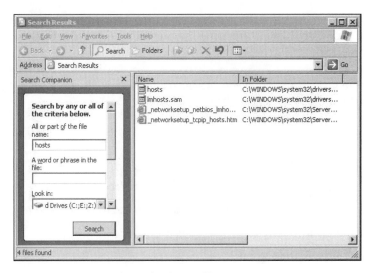

Figure 6-16   Searching for hosts file

6. In the Open With window, select **Notepad** and click **OK**.

7. Add the following line to the end of the file, as shown in Figure 6-17:

   127.0.0.2 www.yahoo.com

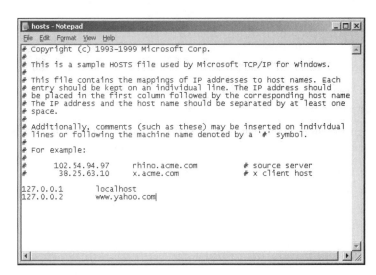

Figure 6-17   Adding line to hosts file

8. Save and close the **hosts** file.

9. Open Internet Explorer and try to go to *www.yahoo.com*.

10. Your computer now thinks that *www.yahoo.com* is located on itself, so it fails to load. If Yahoo does load, it might be in your cache. Click the **Refresh** button to see the error.

TIP

Don't forget to undo these steps before moving on. In other words, delete the line you added to the hosts file, and then resave the file.

To apply this method to pop-ups:

1. When a pop-up appears, right-click it and select **Properties**.

2. Make a note of the server and domain name; for example, *ads.x10.com*.

3. Add the address to the hosts file to prevent pop-ups.

4. Close all windows and log off.

Certification Objectives

Objectives for CompTIA Security+ Exam:

➤ Communication Security: Web

Review Questions

1. The hosts file resolves a(n) _____ .

   a. IP address to host name

   b. IP address to NetBIOS name

   c. IP address to MAC address

   d. host name to IP address

2. You recently made some changes to the hosts file on your computer, but they do not seem to be working. What could be the problem?

   a. The changes were overruled by DNS.

   b. The hosts file is not used if you are configured to use DNS.

   c. You made the changes in a text editor that appended a .txt extension to the file.

   d. You made the changes in a spreadsheet application that appended a .csv extension to the file.

3. You recently changed the IP address of a mail server. Now some remote users cannot access their e-mail. What is the likely cause?

    a. They did not change their e-mail settings to reflect the IP address change.

    b. DNS is not configured properly.

    c. They have an entry in their hosts files with the old IP address.

    d. They deleted their hosts files.

4. Which of the following is an advantage of blocking Web sites with the hosts file?

    a. The site cannot put a cookie on your computer.

    b. It prevents your computer from ever going to the ad servers.

    c. The ad servers cannot profile you.

    d. all of the above

5. A hosts file can increase Web browsing speed. True or False?

6

PROTECTING ADVANCED COMMUNICATIONS

Labs included in this chapter:

➤ Lab 7.1 Enabling Dial-in Access

➤ Lab 7.2 Configuring a Windows Server 2003 VPN Server

➤ Lab 7.3 Using PPTP to Connect to a VPN Server

➤ Lab 7.4 Configuring a Remote Access Policy

➤ Lab 7.5 Configuring a Wireless Access Point

➤ Lab 7.6 Installing the Cisco Aironet 350 Wireless Access Point

➤ Lab 7.7 Disabling Telnet Access to the Aironet WAP

➤ Lab 7.8 Enabling the Aironet User Manager

➤ Lab 7.9 Adding Administrative Users to the Aironet

➤ Lab 7.10 Restoring the Aironet Factory Default Settings

CompTIA Security+ Exam Objectives	
Objective	Lab
Communication Security: Remote Access: VPN	7.1, 7.2, 7.3, 7.4
Communication Security: Remote Access: L2TP/PPTP	7.3
Communication Security: Remote Access: Vulnerabilities	7.4
Communication Security: Remote Access: 802.11, WEP, WAP	7.5
Communication Security: Wireless	7.6, 7.7, 7.8, 7.9, 7.10
Communication Security: Wireless: WEP/WAP	7.6, 7.7, 7.8, 7.9, 7.10

This chapter is organized into two sections. The first section, Labs 7.1 through 7.5, requires the standard equipment listed in the preface of this manual. These labs are required exercises. The second section, Labs 7.6 through 7.10, requires a Cisco Aironet 350 wireless access point. If you have the equipment, we recommend that you complete these labs, but they are not required.

LAB 7.1 ENABLING DIAL-IN ACCESS

Objectives

Remote access to a network is essential for administrators and remote users. Without it, administrators would have to remain in a computer room to do their tasks, and remote users would have to use "snail mail" or fax machines to transfer data. Windows NT/2000/2003 allows remote access, but by default, Windows NT/2000/2003 does not allow dial-in access. The subject of dial-in access includes more than modem access; it also includes VPN access.

After completing this lab, you will be able to:

➤ Edit user properties to grant users dial-in access

➤ Edit user properties to remove dial-in access

Materials Required

This lab requires the following:

➤ A Windows Server 2003 stand-alone server

➤ Administrator access to the server

Estimated completion time: 10 minutes

ACTIVITY

1. Log on as Administrator.

2. Right-click **My Computer** and select **Manage**.

3. Expand **Local Users and Groups** and click **Users**.

4. Double-click **Administrator**.

5. Click the **Dial-in** tab.

6. Select the **Allow access** option, as shown in Figure 7-1.

7. Click **OK**.

8. Close the Computer Management window and log off.

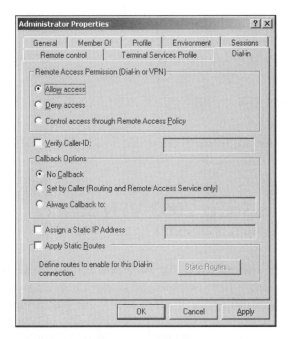

Figure 7-1 Administrator properties

Certification Objectives

Objectives for CompTIA Security+ Exam:

➤ Communication Security: Remote Access: VPN

Review Questions

1. Dial-in access is enabled for the Administrator account only. True or False?

2. Which administrative tool is used to allow dial-in access in a Windows NT environment?

    a. Active Directory Users and Computers

    b. User Manager

    c. Computer Management

    d. Server Manager

3. Which administrative tool is used to allow dial-in access in a Windows Server 2003 workgroup environment?

    a. Active Directory Users and Computers

    b. User Manager

    c. Computer Management

    d. Server Manager

4. Which administrative tool is used to allow dial-in access in a Windows Server 2003 domain environment?

   a. Active Directory Users and Computers

   b. User Manager

   c. Computer Management

   d. Server Manager

5. When dial-in access is enabled, Terminal Services access is also enabled. True or False?

Lab 7.2 Configuring a Windows Server 2003 VPN Server

Objectives

In the past, most companies set up modem pools that were connected to remote access servers to enable remote access for employees. This method worked, but had some short-comings. Modem pools require additional phone lines, plus someone has to support and maintain the modems and phone lines. Given the relative unreliability of modems, this proved to be a problematic solution. Many companies used a third party to supply the phone lines and modems, and to avoid having to support the equipment.

By using virtual private networks (VPNs), a company can replace its modem pool and use in-house staff to support the VPN, thus keeping overhead to a minimum. A VPN uses public Internet connections for private communication. The information transferred over the VPN is kept confidential by using tunneling protocols, which you will learn about in the following labs.

After completing this lab, you will be able to:

➤ Use the Windows Server 2003 Routing and Remote Access Service

➤ Configure a Windows Server 2003 server to accept VPN connections

Materials Required

This lab requires the following:

➤ A Windows Server 2003 stand-alone server

➤ Administrator access to the server

Estimated completion time: 10 minutes

ACTIVITY
LAB ACTIVITY

1. Log on as Administrator. Click **Start**, click **All Programs**, click
    Administrative Tools, and then click **Routing and Remote Access**. Next
    to the server is an icon of a red arrow pointing down, as shown in Figure 7-2.

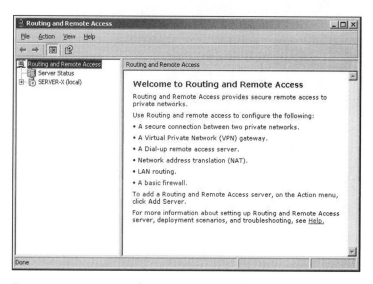

Figure 7-2 Routing and Remote Access window

2. To configure the server, right-click the server name.

3. Select **Configure and Enable Routing and Remote Access**. The Routing
    and Remote Access Server Setup Wizard begins.

4. Click **Next**.

5. Select the **Custom configuration** option, and then click **Next**.

6. Check the **VPN access** check box, as shown in Figure 7-3, and then click
    Next.

7. Click **Finish**.

8. When prompted, click **Yes** to start the Routing and Remote Access Service.

9. Close the Routing and Remote Access window.

10. Log off as Administrator.

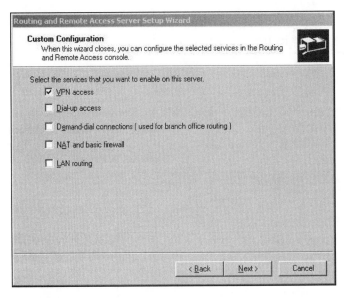

Figure 7-3 Enabling VPN access

Certification Objectives

Objectives for CompTIA Security+ Exam:

➤   Communication Security: Remote Access: VPN

Review Questions

1. Which of the following Windows operating systems support VPN connections? (Choose all that apply.)

   a. Windows NT

   b. Windows 2000/2003

   c. Windows 98

   d. Windows 3.11

2. Which of the following Windows operating systems supports L2TP?

   a. Windows NT

   b. Windows 2000/2003

   c. Windows 98

   d. Windows 3.11

3. Which of the following Windows operating systems can run RRAS?

   a. Windows NT

   b. Windows 2000/2003

   c. Windows 98

   d. Windows 3.11

4. Which of the following Windows operating systems can run a VPN server? (Choose all that apply.)

   a. Windows NT

   b. Windows 2000/2003

   c. Windows 98

   d. Windows 3.11

5. Remote access policies can be configured using Windows Server 2003 Group Policy. True or False?

LAB 7.3 USING PPTP TO CONNECT TO A VPN SERVER

Objectives

Point-to-Point Protocol (PPP) is a remote access protocol that improves on the previous standard, Serial Line Interface Protocol (SLIP). SLIP, the first remote access protocol for TCP/IP, had some major drawbacks. With SLIP, only static IP addresses could be used, and SLIP lacked encryption, compression, and error correction. Using PPP solves all of these problems. Another protocol, PPTP, is a tunneling protocol that uses PPP for encryption. PPTP is the primary protocol used for VPN connections.

After completing this lab, you will be able to:

➤ Set up and enable a dial-up connection to a VPN server using PPTP

Materials Required

This lab requires the following:

➤ Two Windows Server 2003 servers configured as stand-alone servers

➤ One of the servers configured as a VPN server

➤ Administrator access to both servers

Estimated completion time: 15 minutes

LAB ACTIVITY

ACTIVITY

This lab requires two servers. Substitute the names of your servers for Server-X and Server-Y. Server-X signifies the server that should be configured to accept VPN connections.

1. On Server-Y, log on as Administrator. Click **Start**, click **Control Panel**, click **Network Connections**, and then click **New Connection Wizard**.

2. You might be prompted to enter **Location Information**. If so, enter your area code, and then click **OK** twice.

3. Click **Next** in the Network Connection Wizard.

4. Select **Connect to the network at my workplace**, and then click **Next**.

5. Select **Virtual Private Network connection**, and then click **Next**.

6. When prompted to name the connection, name it **PPTP VPN** and click **Next**.

7. Enter Server-X's IP address for the **VPN Server Selection**, and then click **Next**.

8. Check **Anyone's use** in the Connection Availability window, and then click **Next**.

9. Check the **Add a shortcut to this connection to my desktop** option.

10. Click **Finish**. You are automatically prompted to log on.

11. Log on as Administrator. You are now connected.

12. To see what happens if an account does not have dial-in access, go to Server-X and disable dial-in access. Try to connect again. Make sure you re-enable dial-in access if you have disabled it.

13. Close all windows and log off.

Certification Objectives

Objectives for CompTIA Security+ Exam:

➤ Communication Security: Remote Access: VPN

➤ Communication Security: Remote Access: L2TP/PPTP

Review Questions

1. Which of the following is the PPTP control port?

   a. UDP 1723

   b. TCP 1723

   c. TCP 1494

   d. UDP 1494

2. What do the LCP extensions provide for PPTP?

   a. They provide error correction for the data link connection.

   b. They provide Data Link layer tunneling.

   c. They establish, configure, and test the data link connection.

   d. They link and connect the PPTP connection.

3. Which of the following protocols can be used with PPTP? (Choose all that apply.)

   a. IPX/SPX

   b. NetBEUI

   c. TCP/IP

   d. AppleTalk

4. Which protocol does PPTP use for encryption?

   a. PPP

   b. IPSec

   c. ESP

   d. PPTP can encrypt without another protocol.

5. Which of the following operating systems support PPTP? (Choose all that apply.)

   a. Windows Server 2003

   b. Windows NT

   c. Windows 3.11

   d. Windows 9.x

7

Lab 7.4 Configuring a Remote Access Policy

Objectives

Although remote access is an essential tool for today's businesses, it can open a wide range of security holes. One way an administrator can overcome this problem is by using Windows

Server 2003 remote access policies. These policies can lock down a remote access system to ensure that only intended users are actually granted access.

After completing this lab, you will be able to:

➤ Create a remote access policy

Materials Required

This lab requires the following:

➤ Two Windows Server 2003 servers configured as stand-alone servers

➤ Administrator access to both servers

➤ Two user-level accounts: User1 and User2

Estimated completion time:	10 minutes

LAB ACTIVITY

ACTIVITY

This lab requires two servers. Substitute the names of your servers for Server-X and Server-Y.

1. Log on to Server-X as Administrator.

2. Open **Routing and Remote Access** from the Administrative Tools menu.

3. Expand Server-X if necessary by clicking the plus sign (+), and then right-click **Remote Access Policies**.

4. Select **New Remote Access Policy**.

5. Click **Next**.

6. Verify that **Use the wizard to set up a typical policy for a common scenario** is selected, type **Authenticated PPTP Connections** in the Policy name text box, and then click **Next**.

7. Verify that VPN is selected, and then click **Next**.

8. Select **User**, as shown in Figure 7-4. Click **Next**.

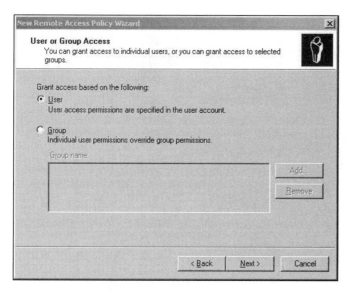

Figure 7-4 Granting users remote access

9. Accept the default authentication method, as shown in Figure 7-5, and then click **Next**.

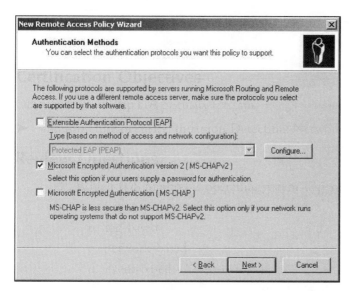

Figure 7-5 Accepting the default authentication method

10. Accept the default policy encryption levels, as shown in Figure 7-6, and then click **Next**.

11. Click **Finish**.

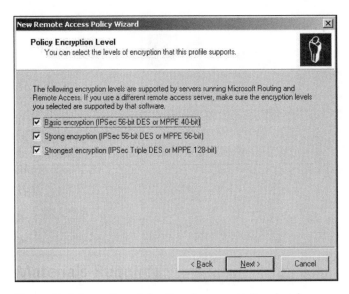

Figure 7-6 Accepting default policy encryption levels

> 12. Click **Remote Access Policies**, as shown in Figure 7-7, to view the existing policies. Note that the policy you just created is the first to be applied.

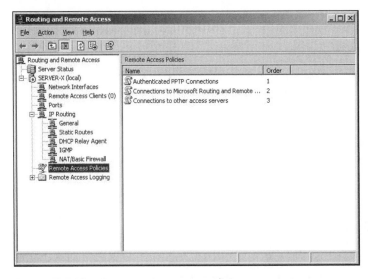

Figure 7-7 Viewing remote access policies

> 13. In **Computer Management**, verify that dial-in access for User1 and User2 is set to **Control access through Remote Access Policy**.

14. Log on to Server-Y and try to access the PPTP VPN connection using User1 or User2 accounts. You will be unsuccessful because of the policy.

15. On Server-X, double-click **Authenticated PPTP Connections** in the Routing and Remote Access window.

16. Edit the remote access policy to **Grant remote access permission**, as shown in Figure 7-8, and then try again to access the PPTP VPN connection from Server-Y. You will be successful.

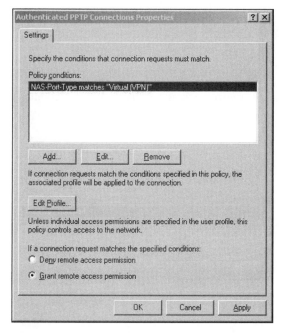

Figure 7-8 Granting remote access permission

Certification Objectives

Objectives for CompTIA Security+ Exam:

➤ Communication Security: Remote Access: VPN

➤ Communication Security: Remote Access: Vulnerabilities

Review Questions

1. The default remote access policy is to allow access if dial-in permission is enabled. True or False?

2. Which of the following is a remote access policy attribute? (Choose all that apply.)

   a. Called-Station-ID

   b. Calling-Station-ID

   c. Client-IP-Address

   d. Tunnel-Type

3. Remote access logging can log which of the following events?

   a. accounting requests

   b. authentication requests

   c. periodic status

   d. all of the above

4. Which of the following can remote access servers provide to clients? (Choose all that apply.)

   a. DHCP

   b. IP spoofing

   c. DHCP relay

   d. DCHP repair

5. The default maximum port limit for each device that supports multiple ports is _____ .

   a. 1

   b. 0

   c. 256

   d. 128

LAB 7.5 CONFIGURING A WIRELESS ACCESS POINT

Objectives

In the past, wireless technologies were recognized more for their convenience than their security. In fact, wireless access opened security holes that were once unknown to IT security professionals—an intruder no longer had to enter a corporate building to gain access to a company's network. For this reason, many businesses decide not to use wireless access. Wireless technologies have added security features that reduce the risk of intrusion, but there are still weaknesses.

After completing this lab, you will be able to:

➤ Configure a Microsoft wireless base station

Materials Required

This lab requires the following:

➤ A Windows Server 2003 server or Windows 2000/XP PC

➤ A Microsoft MN-700 broadband networking wireless base station

Estimated completion time: 30 minutes

LAB ACTIVITY

ACTIVITY

7

1. Install the MN-700 software. Connect the MN-700 to a power source and then connect it to the network card of your server.

   To install the MN-700 software, insert the setup CD. If the setup program does not start automatically, run setup.exe from the CD. Select **Install software only**, and then click **Next**. If prompted to install DirectX, check the box to install it, and then click **Next**. Accept the license agreement, click **Next**, and then click **Finish**. After the system restarts, log on as Administrator. When the wizard starts automatically, accept the license agreement and the default installation folder, and then click **Finish**. Close the Broadband Network Utility window, which displays the network status..

2. Start **Internet Explorer**.

3. Enter **http://192.168.2.1** in the **Address** text box.

4. Type **admin** (or your current password) for the password, and then click **Log On**, as shown in Figure 7-9. A summary window similar to that shown in Figure 7-10 appears.

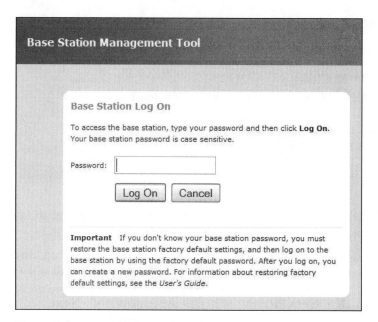

Figure 7-9 Logging on as Administrator

5. To change the password, click **Management** and then click **Change Password**. A window similar to that shown in Figure 7-11 appears.

6. Type **admin** (or your current password) in the **Current password** text box.

7. Type **password** in the **New password (3–16 characters)** text box.

8. Type **password** in the **Confirm new password** text box.

9. Click **Apply**.

10. To set the wireless settings, click the **Wireless** link.

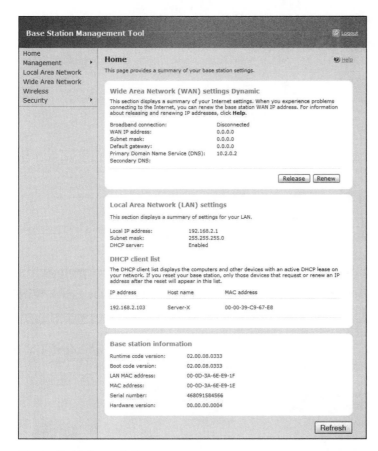

Figure 7-10 Base station summary

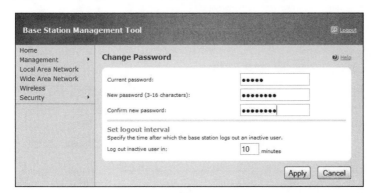

Figure 7-11 Changing the base station password

11. Change the settings as shown in Figure 7-12. Replace the X in Course-X with your server number.

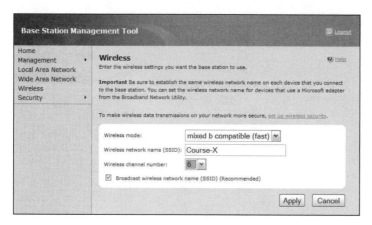

Figure 7-12 Changing the base station wireless settings

12. Click **Apply**, and then click **OK** in response to the next prompt.

13. To configure the security settings, click **Security** and then click **Wireless Security**.

14. Change the settings as shown in Figure 7-13. You might want to choose a more secure encryption method outside of the lab environment. But be aware that as the encryption increases, performance decreases.

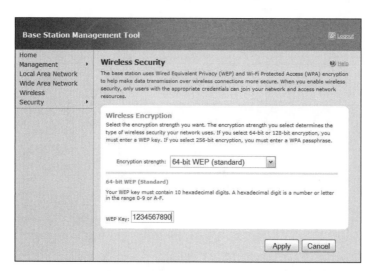

Figure 7-13 Changing the base station wireless security settings

15. Click **Apply**. You see the message shown in Figure 7-14.

16. Click **OK**. You are prompted to log on again because the device must reset.

17. To set the base station to Access Point mode, log on to the access point.

Figure 7-14 Notification that wireless security settings have changed

18. Click the **Security** link, and then click **Base Station Mode**.

19. Change the settings as shown in Figure 7-15. Replace the X in Course-X with your server number.

7

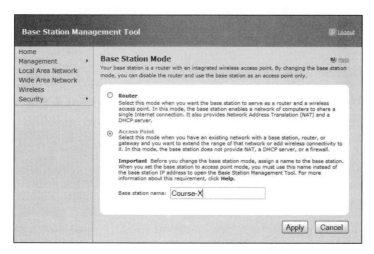

Figure 7-15 Changing base station mode settings

20. Click **Apply**. You see the message shown in Figure 7-16.

Figure 7-16 Confirming change to Access Point mode

21. Click **OK**. You see the message shown in Figure 7-17.

22. Click **OK**. The access point is ready to use. Close any open windows, disconnect all cables, and reconnect your server to the network.

Figure 7-17 Notification that the base station must restart

Certification Objectives

Objectives for CompTIA Security+ Exam:

➤ Communication Security: Remote Access: 802.11, WEP, WAP

Review Questions

1. The wireless network name is case sensitive. True or False?

2. What is the maximum number of characters in a network name?

    a. 10

    b. 32

    c. 64

    d. 128

3. The wireless network name is also known as an SSID. What does SSID mean?

    a. secure server identifier

    b. service set identifier

    c. secure shell identifier

    d. service store identifier

4. What is the default encryption strength of the Microsoft MN-700?

    a. 64-bit

    b. 128-bit

    c. 256-bit

    d. none

5. 128-bit WEP is considered _____ .

    a. weak

    b. strong

    c. very strong

    d. impenetrable

LAB 7.6 INSTALLING THE CISCO AIRONET 350 WIRELESS ACCESS POINT

Objectives

Access to a network is essential for most employees in companies, particularly for IT professionals. For IT professionals who use a laptop computer in multiple locations, a network connection is not always available. In these cases, wireless access is a convenient tool. In this lab you will install the Cisco Aironet 350 wireless access point (WAP), which allows laptops and other mobile computer systems wireless access to a network.

After completing this lab, you will be able to:

➤ Install a Cisco Aironet 350 wireless access point

➤ Configure the SSID and Radio Channel for the Cisco Aironet 350 WAP

Materials Required

This lab requires the following:

➤ A Windows Server 2003 server with Administrator access

➤ A Cisco Aironet 350 WAP

Estimated completion time: 20–25 minutes

ACTIVITY

1. Connect the Cisco Aironet 350 to a power source and then connect it to your Ethernet-based network.

2. Identify the MAC address assigned to the Aironet device. You can find the MAC address on the bottom of the Aironet.

3. Ask the instructor what IP address is assigned to the MAC address of your Aironet.

4. If you are running DHCP on your server, check the **Unique ID** column in the DHCP Manager for the MAC address, as shown in Figure 7-18. Note that you might have to scroll to the right to see the column.

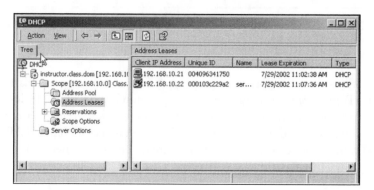

Figure 7-18 Checking the unique ID

5. Log on to your server as Administrator and start **Internet Explorer**.

6. Enter the IP address of the Aironet in the **Address** text box, and then press **Enter**. You should see the window shown in Figure 7-19.

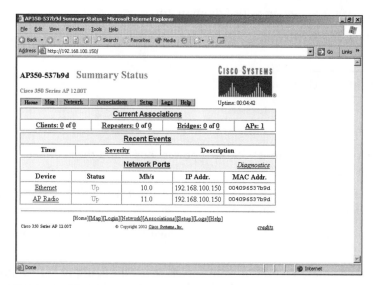

Figure 7-19 Cisco Aironet 350 Summary Status window

7. Click the **AP Radio** link. You see a window similar to the one shown in Figure 7-20.

8. Click the **Set Properties** link. You see a window similar to the one shown in Figure 7-21.

9. Note that the default SSID is **tsunami**. To assign a unique identity to this WLAN, change this value to your last name.

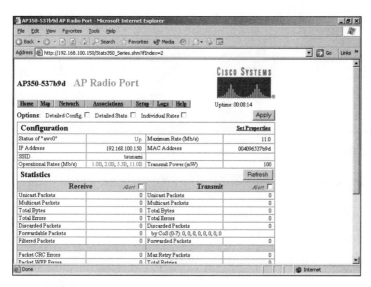

Figure 7-20 Cisco Aironet 350 AP Radio Port information

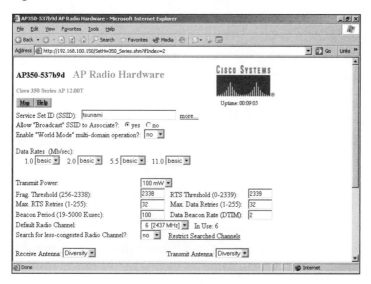

Figure 7-21 Cisco Aironet 350 AP Radio Hardware information

10. Note the Default Radio Channel. If you have a 2.4-GHz cordless phone, the channels can interfere with each other. You can adjust this value to any number from 1 through 11.

11. Scroll down if necessary, and then click **OK**. You might receive the message shown in Figure 7-22. If so, click the **here** link to force the window to refresh its display.

12. Click **OK** and close your Web browser.

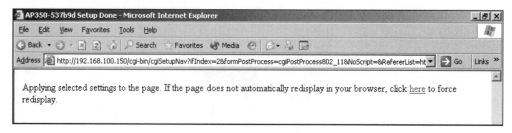

Figure 7-22 Notification that settings are being applied

Certification Objectives

Objectives for CompTIA Security+ Exam:

➤   Communication Security: Wireless

➤   Communication Security: Wireless: WEP/WAP

Review Questions

1. Which of the following can you use to access the Cisco Aironet WAP?

    a. Telnet

    b. serial

    c. Ethernet

    d. HTTP

    e. all of the above

2. Which of the following requires direct access to the Cisco Aironet WAP?

    a. Telnet

    b. serial

    c. Ethernet

    d. HTTP

3. The default configuration of the Cisco Aironet allows everyone access to the system configuration. True or False?

4. Which of the following is a setting used for terminal connections? (Choose all that apply.)

    a. 8 data bits

    b. 9600 bits per second

    c. 1 stop bit

    d. no parity

    e. XON/XOFF flow control

5. The Cisco Aironet can operate at 2.4 GHz and can conflict with certain cordless phones. True or False?

LAB 7.7 DISABLING TELNET ACCESS TO THE AIRONET WAP

Objectives

Telnet is a very useful TCP/IP utility, but it has security holes. One major security flaw is that it sends passwords across the wire in plaintext. To be safe, you can disable Telnet directly from the Cisco Aironet. This makes administration a little more difficult because you are removing a method of administrative access, but it helps to further secure the device. HTTP access will be available as an administrative access method once this lab is complete.

After completing this lab, you will be able to:

➤ Access the Cisco Aironet Setup window

➤ Disable Telnet access to the WAP

Materials Required

This lab requires the following:

➤ A Windows Server 2003 server with Administrator access

➤ A Cisco Aironet 350 WAP

Estimated completion time: 10–15 minutes

ACTIVITY

1. On your server, click **Start**, click **Run**, and type **cmd** at the command line. Press **Enter**.

2. Enter **telnet xx.xx.xx.xx**, where the **xx** symbols represent the actual address of your Aironet.

3. Press **Enter**. Note that you were able to connect.

4. Close the command window.

5. Start **Internet Explorer**.

6. Enter the IP address of the Aironet in the **Address** text box, and then press **Enter**.

7. Click the **Setup** link to enter the Setup window (see Figure 7-23).

8. Under Services, click the **Console/Telnet** link.

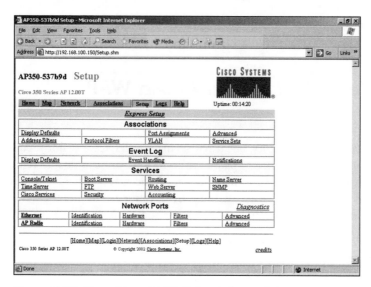

Figure 7-23 Cisco Aironet 350 Setup information

9. Click the **Disabled** option, as shown in Figure 7-24.

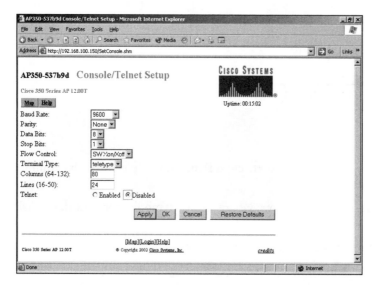

Figure 7-24 Cisco Aironet 350 Console/Telnet Setup information

10. Click **OK**. You might receive the message shown in Figure 7-25. If so, click the **here** link to force the window to refresh its display. The setting is saved, and you return to the Setup window.

11. Click **Start**, click **Run**, and type **cmd** at the command line. Press **Enter**.

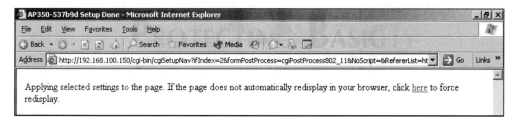

Figure 7-25 Notification that settings are being applied

12. Enter **telnet *xx.xx.xx.xx***, where the ***xx*** symbols represent the actual address of your Aironet, and then press **Enter**. Telnet access is disabled.

13. Close the command window, and then close **Internet Explorer**.

Certification Objectives

Objectives for CompTIA Security+ Exam:

➤ Communication Security: Wireless

➤ Communication Security: Wireless: WEP/WAP

Review Questions

1. Which of the following can you use to configure the Cisco Aironet in a text-based environment?

   a. Telnet

   b. FTP

   c. TFTP

   d. HTTP

2. Which of the following can you use to configure the Cisco Aironet in a GUI environment?

   a. Telnet

   b. FTP

   c. TFTP

   d. HTTP

3. Telnet is disabled by default on the Cisco Aironet. True or False?

4. Telnet can be a security risk because it transmits the username and password in plaintext. True or False?

5. Which of the following TCP ports does Telnet use?

   a. 20

   b. 21

   c. 23

   d. 25

LAB 7.8 ENABLING THE AIRONET USER MANAGER

Objectives

The default setting of the Cisco Aironet 350 is to allow all users access to the configuration utilities, which is convenient for initial setup and configuration. Once the device is ready for production, however, you should control access. If you fail to change this configuration, you run the risk of handing a cracker the key to your wireless network. To limit access to the configuration utilities, you must enable the User Manager, change the Administrator password, and add more accounts. Remember that the account names are case sensitive and that if you forget the passwords, you will have to use the serial port access to reset the device.

After completing this lab, you will be able to:

➤ Enable the Cisco Aironet 350 WAP User Manager

➤ Configure password access to the Cisco Aironet 350 WAP

Materials Required

This lab requires the following:

➤ A Windows Server 2003 server with Administrator access

➤ A Cisco Aironet 350 WAP

Estimated completion time: 10–15 minutes

ACTIVITY

1. Start **Internet Explorer**. Click **Tools** on the menu bar, click **Internet Options**, and then click the **Security** tab. Click the **Custom Level** button and make sure **Active Scripting** is **enabled**.

2. Enter the IP address of the Aironet in the **Address** text box, and then press **Enter**.

3. Click the **Setup** link.

4. Under Services, click the **Security** link. You see the window shown in Figure 7-26.

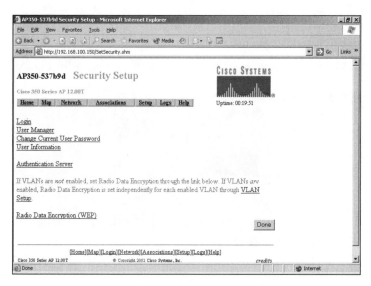

Figure 7-26 Cisco Aironet 350 Security Setup information

5. Click the **User Information** link.

6. Click the **Administrator** link.

7. Set the username to **Administrator** and the password to **password**.

8. Select all of the options under the **capability settings**, as shown in Figure 7-27.

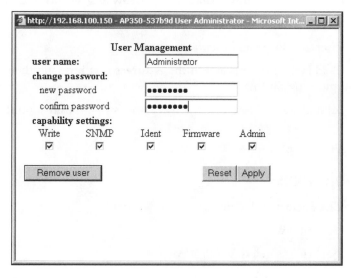

Figure 7-27 Setting User Management capabilities

9. Click **Apply**.

10. Click the **Back** button in Internet Explorer.

11. Click the **User Manager** link. You see the window shown in Figure 7-28.

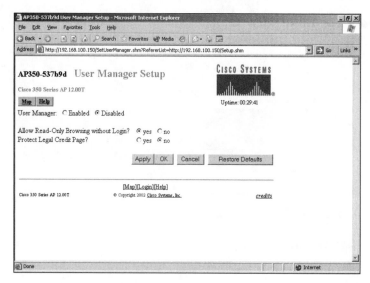

Figure 7-28 User Manager Setup information

12. Click the **Enabled** option to enable the User Manager.

13. Click the **no** option for **Allow Read-Only Browsing without Login?**.

14. Click **OK**. When you are prompted to accept the changes, click **OK** again.

15. Close **Internet Explorer** and then restart it.

16. Enter the IP address of the Aironet in the **Address** text box, and then press **Enter**. You must log on to access the Aironet settings.

17. Log on as Administrator. Note that the username is case sensitive on this device.

18. Close **Internet Explorer**.

Certification Objectives

Objectives for CompTIA Security+ Exam:

➤ Communication Security: Wireless

➤ Communication Security: Wireless: WEP/WAP

Review Questions

1. When limiting access to configuration utilities, which of the following should be changed, besides adding users? (Choose all that apply.)

   a. the MAC address

   b. the default account and password

   c. the IP address

   d. the SSID

2. One way to secure a wireless network is to use a _____ .

   a. firewall

   b. scrambler

   c. VPN

   d. DMZ

3. One way to secure the wireless administration of a Cisco Aironet is to _____ .

   a. disable access to the WAP

   b. disable a router

   c. disable administrative access to the WAP

   d. disable security settings on the WAP

4. A recommended practice for wireless LANs is to _____ .

   a. disable file and printer sharing

   b. disable NetBEUI

   c. enable WEP protection

   d. use a nonobvious encryption key

   e. all of the above

5. Which of the following can interfere with wireless transmission? (Choose all that apply.)

   a. brick walls

   b. cell phones

   c. cordless phones

   d. distance

Lab 7.9 Adding Administrative Users to the Aironet

Objectives

As discussed in Lab 7.8, you can add users with the Aironet User Manager. This is useful if you plan to log events, including configuration changes. One common mistake that companies make is to share the Administrator password with all administrators. This is not a good practice, because you can never be sure which administrator has made changes to the configuration. Each administrator that must have access to this device should use a unique username and password, so that you can keep track of who is making changes.

After completing this lab, you will be able to:

➤ Allow users to access the Aironet configuration

➤ Grant permissions to new users

Materials Required

This lab requires the following:

➤ A Windows Server 2003 server with Administrator access

➤ A Cisco Aironet 350 WAP

Estimated completion time: 10–15 minutes

Activity

1. Start **Internet Explorer**.

2. Enter the IP address of the Aironet in the **Address** text box, and then press **Enter**.

3. Log on as Administrator.

4. Click the **Setup** link.

5. Under Services, click the **Security** link.

6. Click **User Information**.

7. Click the **Add New User** button.

8. Enter your name and choose a password.

9. Click the following options under the capability settings: **Write**, **Firmware**, and **Admin**, as shown in Figure 7-29.

10. Click **Apply**.

11. Close **Internet Explorer** and then restart it.

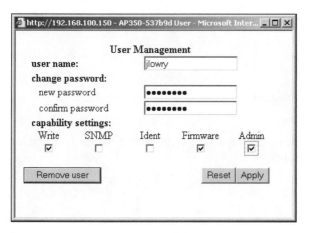

Figure 7-29 Setting user capabilities

12. Enter the IP address of the Aironet in the **Address** text box, and then press **Enter**.

13. Log on with your new account information.

14. Click **Setup**.

15. Under Services, click **Console/Telnet**.

16. Click the **Enabled** option.

17. Click **Apply**.

18. Click **OK** and close **Internet Explorer**.

Certification Objectives

Objectives for CompTIA Security+ Exam:

➤ Communication Security: Wireless

➤ Communication Security: Wireless: WEP/WAP

Review Questions

1. Administrators should use a separate account because it makes the system more secure. True or False?

2. Administrators should use a separate account because it makes auditing easier and more reliable. True or False?

3. The Cisco Aironet application used to administer access is called
   _____ .

   a. Server Manager

   b. User Manager

   c. Computer Management

   d. WAP Manager

4. Which of the following are capability settings available to user accounts? (Choose all that apply.)

   a. Write

   b. SNMP

   c. Firmware

   d. Admin

5. To enable User Manager, at least one account must have full power. True or False?

LAB 7.10 RESTORING THE AIRONET FACTORY DEFAULT SETTINGS

Objectives

In this lab, you will restore the factory default settings to the Aironet to undo the changes you made during Labs 7.6 through 7.9. This is a good practice when you install a device out of the box, because you can never be sure if the box was opened, the unit used, and then returned.

After completing this lab, you will be able to:

➤ Reset the Aironet settings to the factory defaults

➤ Undo the changes made to the Cisco Aironet during Labs 7.6 through 7.9

Materials Required

This lab requires the following:

➤ A Windows Server 2003 server with Administrator access

➤ A Cisco Aironet 350 WAP

Estimated completion time: 15 minutes

ACTIVITY

1. Start **Internet Explorer**.

2. Enter the IP address of the Aironet in the **Address** text box, and then press **Enter**.

3. Log on as Administrator.

4. Click the **Setup** link.

5. Click the **Security** link.

6. Click **User Manager**.

7. **Disable** User Manager.

8. Click **OK**, and then click **OK** again. You might need to click the **here** link to force the window to redisplay.

9. Click the **Setup** link.

10. Under Services, click the **Cisco Services** link. The window shown in Figure 7-30 appears.

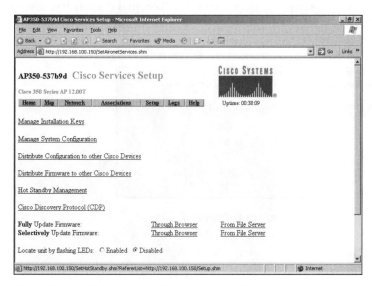

Figure 7-30 Cisco Services Setup information

11. Click the **Manage System Configuration** link. The window shown in Figure 7-31 appears.

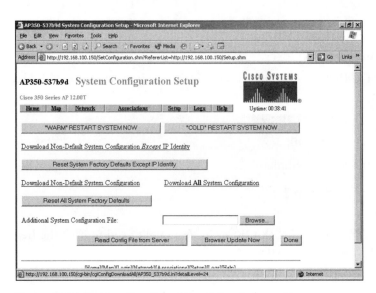

Figure 7-31 System Configuration Setup information

12. Click **Reset System Factory Defaults Except IP Identity**. This resets all devices, except for the IP address, and any accounts you created. You receive the message shown in Figure 7–32.

Figure 7-32 Confirming system reset to factory defaults

13. Click **OK**. After 30 seconds or so, you receive the message shown in Figure 7-33.

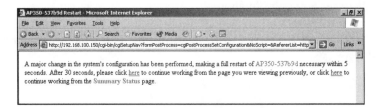

Figure 7-33 Notification that system must restart

14. Close **Internet Explorer**, and then start it again.

15. Enter the IP address of the Aironet in the **Address** text box, and then press **Enter**. You should not be prompted to log on. You see the Express Setup window, as shown in Figure 7-34.

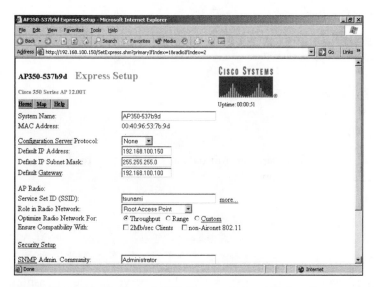

Figure 7-34 Cisco Aironet 350 Express Setup information

16. Close all open windows.

Certification Objectives

Objectives for CompTIA Security+ Exam:

➤ Communication Security: Wireless

➤ Communication Security: Wireless: WEP/WAP

Review Questions

1. The 802.11a standard can use which of the following bands?

   a. 2.4 GHz

   b. 5 GHz

   c. 2.4 MHz

   d. 5 MHz

2. The 802.11b standard uses which of the following bands?

    a. 2.4 GHz

    b. 5 GHz

    c. 2.4 MHz

    d. 5 MHz

3. The 802.11a standard can transmit data at speeds of up to
    _____ Mbps.

    a. 11

    b. 36

    c. 48

    d. 54

4. The 802.11b standard can transmit data at speeds of up to
    _____ Mbps.

    a. 11

    b. 36

    c. 48

    d. 54

5. Which of the following protocols is used to encrypt wireless transmission?

    a. WAP

    b. WEP

    c. WSP

    d. WDP

8

SCRAMBLING THROUGH CRYPTOGRAPHY

Labs included in this chapter:

➤ Lab 8.1 Using NTFS to Secure Local Resources

➤ Lab 8.2 Ensuring Data Confidentiality

➤ Lab 8.3 Ensuring Data Availability

➤ Lab 8.4 Ensuring Data Integrity

➤ Lab 8.5 Encrypting Data

CompTIA Security+ Exam Objectives	
Objective	Lab
General Security Concepts: Access Control	8.1, 8.2, 8.3, 8.4, 8.5

LAB 8.1 USING NTFS TO SECURE LOCAL RESOURCES

Objectives

Local computer security is often ignored, especially at the file level. Most people are familiar with the Windows 9x version of Microsoft Windows, which uses FAT and does not offer local file security. NTFS, the file system for Windows NT/2000/2003, is designed with local file security in mind. To take advantage of these capabilities, you must have Windows NT, 2000, or XP with the NTFS file system installed. Although all of these operating systems are compatible with FAT, local file security is enabled only if you have NTFS installed.

After completing this lab, you will be able to:

➤ Determine if a partition is FAT or NTFS

➤ Convert a FAT partition to NTFS

Materials Required

This lab requires the following:

➤ A computer running Windows Server 2003 as a stand-alone or member server

➤ Administrative access to the server

➤ At least one partition formatted with FAT or FAT32

Estimated completion time: 10 minutes

ACTIVITY

1. Log on to the Windows Server 2003 server as Administrator.

2. Click **Start**, click **All Programs**, click **Accessories**, and then click **Command Prompt**.

The FAT partition in this lab will be designated as drive letter E.

3. At the command line, type **chkntfs e:** and then press **Enter** to verify that the drive is not using NTFS. You should see the message "E: is not dirty". This means that the drive has no corruption.

4. At the command line, type **convert e: /fs:ntfs** and then press **Enter** to convert the FAT partition to NTFS.

5. If the drive has a volume label, enter it when prompted. Windows converts the drive to NTFS. Note that if you convert the system partition, you must restart the computer for the conversion to take place.

6. At the command line, type **chkntfs e:** and then press **Enter** to verify that the drive is now NTFS. An example of the preceding steps is shown in Figure 8-1.

8

Figure 8-1   Verifying that the drive is NTFS

7. Close all windows and log off.

Certification Objectives

Objectives for CompTIA Security+ Exam:

➤   General Security Concepts: Access Control

Review Questions

1. What file systems are compatible with Windows NT Server 4.0? (Choose all that apply.)

   a. FAT

   b. FAT32

   c. OSPF

   d. NTFS

2. Which of the following are features of NTFS version 5 that are not available with FAT partitions? (Choose all that apply.)

   a. share-level security

   b. file-level security

   c. compression

   d. encryption

3. Which of the following commands converts a FAT partition to NTFS?

   a. update C: /FS:NTFS

   b. upgrade C: /FS:NTFS

   c. convert C: /FS:NTFS

   d. convert C: /NTFS

4. What permissions are available for Windows folder shares? (Choose all that apply.)

   a. Read

   b. Modify

   c. Change

   d. Full Control

5. Once a FAT partition has been converted to NTFS, the only way to change it back to FAT is to rebuild the drive and restore it from a backup. True or False?

Lab 8.2 Ensuring Data Confidentiality

Objectives

Once a secure file system is installed, you can begin to think about data confidentiality. Data confidentiality refers to making sure that only users who are intended to have access to certain data actually have access. With the FAT file system, this confidentiality is not possible at the local level, but with NTFS you can lock down both folders and files locally. NTFS can be used to protect data from intruders who might have physical access to the computer containing the data. In this lab, you will create a folder and files, assign NTFS permissions, and then verify whether the data is confidential.

After completing this lab, you will be able to:

➤ Assign NTFS permissions to a folder and files to secure local resources

➤ Verify that the data is confidential

Materials Required

This lab requires the following:

➤ Completion of Lab 8.1

➤ A computer running Windows Server 2003 as a stand-alone or member server

➤ Administrative access to the server

➤ An NTFS partition

➤ A user-level account named User1

| Estimated completion time: 10 minutes |

ACTIVITY

1. Log on to the Windows Server 2003 server as Administrator.

2. Open **My Computer**, and then double-click the **E:** drive. This should be the drive you converted from FAT to NTFS in Lab 8.1.

3. Create a folder called **Confidentiality**.

4. Create a folder within the **Confidentiality** folder. Name this folder **User1Folder**.

5. To secure this folder from other users, right-click **User1Folder**.

6. Click **Properties** to open the User1Folder Properties window.

7. Click the **Security** tab, as shown in Figure 8-2. Note that if the drive was not formatted with NTFS, the Security tab is unavailable.

8. Click the **Advanced** button, and then uncheck the box labeled **Allow inheritable permissions from the parent to propagate to this object and all child objects**. You see the message shown in Figure 8-3.

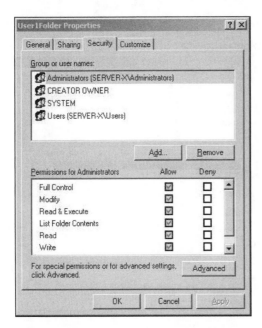

Figure 8-2   User security properties

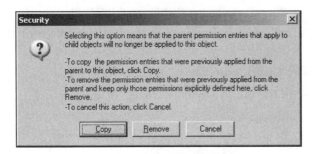

Figure 8-3   Parent and child permission message

9. Click **Copy** to retain the permissions.

10. Click **Add**; the Select User or Group window appears.

11. Make sure your server is selected in the **From this location** list box.

12. Enter **User1** in the **Enter the object name to select** text box, and click **OK**.

13. With User1 still highlighted, click the **Allow Full Control** option in the Permissions section, and then click **OK** twice.

14. Click the **Users** group, and then click **Remove**. Repeat this step for the Administrators, CREATOR OWNER, and SYSTEM accounts. The screen should resemble Figure 8-4.

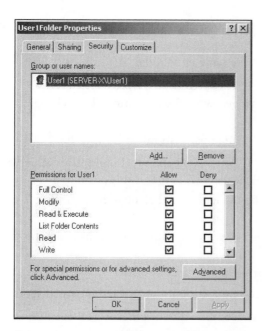

Figure 8-4   Ensuring data confidentiality

15. Click **OK**.

16. Double-click **User1Folder**. Your access is denied because you only granted User1 access.

17. Close all windows and log off.

18. Log on as User1 and navigate to the User1Folder to verify that the user has access to the folder. You will be able to access the folder.

19. Close all windows and log off.

Certification Objectives

Objectives for CompTIA Security+ Exam:

➤   General Security Concepts: Access Control

Review Questions

1. Data confidentiality is best defined as _____ .

    a. data that has not been tampered with intentionally or accidentally

    b. data that has been scrambled for remote transmission

    c. data that is secured so only intended users have access

    d. data that can be accessed when it is needed

2. When comparing the Full Control and Modify NTFS permissions, what differentiates the two?

    a. Full Control is exactly the same as Modify.

    b. Full Control allows you to change permissions and ownership.

    c. Modify only allows changes, while Full Control allows changes as well as deletions.

    d. Modify allows you to change permissions and ownership.

3. A safeguard in Windows NT/2000/2003 allows administrators to access data even if they have been explicitly denied. How is this possible?

    a. Administrators can take ownership and change the permissions to allow access.

    b. Administrators can log on as a user with permissions and grant themselves access.

    c. Administrators cannot be denied access to data.

    d. This safeguard does not exist; administrators can be denied access to data.

4. When NTFS permissions are combined with other NTFS permissions, what are the effective permissions?

    a. most restrictive

    b. least restrictive

5. When NTFS permissions are combined with share permissions, what are the effective permissions?

    a. most restrictive

    b. least restrictive

LAB 8.3 ENSURING DATA AVAILABILITY

Objectives

Although it is important that data remains secure and confidential, it is just as important that the data is available when needed. When secured data is inaccessible, it is considered as downtime, which is detrimental to a business and its ability to serve customers. Technologies such as clustering and load balancing can help, but if NTFS permissions are assigned inappropriately, these features will not help.

After completing this lab, you will be able to:

➤ Share data so that it is available to those who require access

➤ Understand how confidentiality and availability work together

Materials Required

This lab requires the following:

➤ Completion of Lab 8.1

➤ A computer running Windows Server 2003 as a stand-alone or member server

➤ Administrative access to the server

➤ An NTFS partition

➤ A user-level account named User2

Estimated completion time: 10 minutes

8

ACTIVITY

1. Log on to the Windows Server 2003 server as Administrator.

2. Open **My Computer**, and then double-click the **E:** drive.

3. Create a folder called **Availability**.

4. Create a folder within the **Availability** folder. Name this folder **User2Folder**.

5. Right-click **User2Folder**.

6. Click **Properties** to open the User2Folder Properties window.

7. Click the **Security** tab, and then click the **Advanced** button.

8. Uncheck the box labeled **Allow inheritable permissions from the parent to propagate to this object and all child objects**.

9. When prompted to Copy, Remove, or Cancel, click **Remove** to clear the permissions.

10. Click **Add**; the Select User or Group window opens.

11. Make sure your server is selected in the **From this location** list box.

12. Enter **User2** in the **Enter the object name to select** text box, and click **OK**.

13. With User2 still highlighted, click the **Allow Full Control** option in the Permissions section.

14. Click **OK** three times.

15. Close all windows and log off.

16. Log on as User2 and verify that you have access to **E:\Availability\ User2Folder**.

17. Close all windows and log off.

18. Log on as Administrator and delete the **User2** account from the local security database.

19. Create a new user, also named **User2**, and then log off.

20. Log on as User2 and try to access **E:\Availability\User2Folder**. Access should be denied.

21. Log off as User2.

22. Log on as Administrator.

23. Check the **Security properties** of **E:\Availability\User2Folder**. Notice that the account is no longer listed, but the old SID (security identifier) is. Your properties should look like those in Figure 8-5.

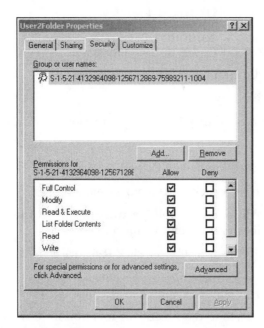

Figure 8-5   Ensuring data availability

24. Close all windows and log off.

Certification Objectives

Objectives for CompTIA Security+ Exam:

➤   General Security Concepts: Access Control

Review Questions

1. Data availability is best defined as _____ .

   a. data that has not been tampered with intentionally or accidentally

   b. data that has been scrambled for remote transmission

   c. data that is secured so only intended users have access

   d. data that can be accessed when it is needed

2. What technologies can be used to help reduce downtime and increase the time that data is readily available? (Choose all that apply.)

   a. backups

   b. clustering

   c. load balancing

   d. RAID

3. A user took a leave of absence from your company for personal reasons. A junior administrator deleted the user's account from Active Directory. To fix the problem, the junior administrator re-created the account. When the user returned to work, he could not access any of his files. What is the cause?

   a. Accounts with the same name should work; that is not the cause of the problem.

   b. The user's account had expired.

   c. The user's password did not comply with the domain security policy.

   d. Even though the two accounts have the same name, the SIDs are different.

4. How can data confidentiality affect data availability?

   a. They are two independent areas that do not affect each other.

   b. For data to be available, it cannot be confidential.

   c. Data that is secured too strongly might conflict with the availability.

   d. Data that is secured too weakly might conflict with the availability.

5. What percentage of downtime would be acceptable for an e-commerce business?

   a. 95%

   b. 100%

   c. 0%

   d. 50%

8

LAB 8.4 ENSURING DATA INTEGRITY

Objectives

Once data is secured properly and is available to the appropriate people, it is important to make sure that the contents of the data have not been altered accidentally or intentionally. Malicious corruption is a problem, and can be inflicted by a virus, worm, or hacker. Accidental changes, however, can also damage data integrity. For example, Windows Server 2003 file synchronization capabilities could easily lead to accidental corruption. Changes made to data that conflict with other changes to the same data can damage data integrity just as much as a hacker.

After completing this lab, you will be able to:

➤ Understand the importance of data integrity

➤ Identify potential threats to data integrity

Materials Required

This lab requires the following:

➤ A computer running Windows Server 2003 as a stand-alone or member server

➤ An NTFS partition

➤ Two user-level accounts: User1 and User2

Estimated completion time: 10 minutes

ACTIVITY

1. Log on to the Windows Server 2003 server as User1.

2. Open **My Computer**, and then double-click the **E:** drive.

3. Create a folder called **Integrity**.

4. Create a folder within the **Integrity** folder. Name this folder **User1Folder**.

5. Right-click **User1Folder**, select **Properties**, and then click the **Security** tab. Highlight **Users**, grant users **Modify** permission by clicking the **Modify Allow** option, and click **OK**. This is necessary because Windows Server 2003 does not offer "Everyone, Full Control" as a default setting, unlike previous versions.

6. Double-click the **User1Folder** folder.

7. Create a text document that contains the following text: **This document has not been modified accidentally or intentionally.**

8. Save the file as **New Text Document.txt** and close the document.

9. Log off as User1.

10. Log on as User2.

11. Navigate to **E:\Integrity\User1Folder** and remove the word "**not**" from the New Text Document. Because you assigned the Modify permission to E:\Integrity\User1Folder, you can modify the contents of the file.

12. Close the file and save the changes.

13. Log off as User2.

Certification Objectives

Objectives for CompTIA Security+ Exam:

➤ General Security Concepts: Access Control

Review Questions

1. Data integrity is best defined as _____ .

    a. data that has not been tampered with intentionally or accidentally

    b. data that has been scrambled for remote transmission

    c. data that is secured so only intended users have access

    d. data that can be accessed when it is needed

2. Data integrity can be damaged by which of the following? (Choose all that apply.)

    a. viruses

    b. worms

    c. hackers

    d. Trojan horses

3. An administrator restores a folder of files at the request of the folder's owner. Two days later the user calls the Help desk to complain that some data is missing from files that were updated two weeks ago. What could have happened?

    a. The restore failed and corrupted the data.

    b. The restore was successful but restored some files that should not have been restored.

    c. The original backup was corrupt.

    d. The user's files were infected with a virus.

4. Data integrity can be threatened by environmental hazards such as dust, surges, and excessive heat. True or False?

5. Which of the following helps maintain data integrity? (Choose all that apply.)

    a. disaster recovery plans

    b. an equipment standards policy

    c. system documentation

    d. preventive maintenance

LAB 8.5 ENCRYPTING DATA

Objectives

With NTFS you are not limited to folder-level and file-level security. Another function of NTFS is the ability to encrypt data. Encryption is the process of taking readable data and making it unreadable. Encryption is commonly used for remote data transfer, but it can also be used for local security. Laptop users might want to use NTFS to secure and encrypt their data in the event the laptop is stolen. While this solution is not 100% effective, it makes hacking more difficult. Windows Server 2003 offers an easy way to encrypt files on an NTFS partition.

After completing this lab, you will be able to:

➤ Encrypt files on NTFS partitions

➤ Understand who has access to encrypted data

Materials Required

This lab requires the following:

➤ A computer running Windows Server 2003 as a stand-alone or member server

➤ Administrative access to the server

➤ An NTFS partition

➤ Two user-level accounts: User1 and User2

Estimated completion time: 10 minutes

ACTIVITY

1. Log on to the Windows Server 2003 server as Administrator.

2. Open **My Computer**, and then double-click the **E:** drive.

3. Create a folder called **Encryption**.

4. Create a folder within the **Encryption** folder. Name this folder **User2Folder**.

5. Double-click the **User2Folder** folder.

6. Create a text document that contains the following text: **This document is for my eyes only.**

7. Save the document as **Private Document.txt** and close it.

8. Right-click the document.

9. Select **Properties**.

10. Click the **Advanced** button.

11. Check the **Encrypt contents to secure data** option, as shown in Figure 8-6.

Figure 8-6   Encrypting data

12. Click **OK**.

13. Click **OK** again. You receive the warning message shown in Figure 8-7.

Figure 8-7   Encryption warning

14. Click the **Encrypt the file only** option.

15. Click **OK**.

16. Log off as Administrator and log on as User1.

17. Try to access Private Document.txt in E:\Encryption\User2Folder. Access should be denied, even though the Users group has NTFS Read permission.

18. Log off as User1.

Certification Objectives

Objectives for CompTIA Security+ Exam:

➤ General Security Concepts: Access Control

Review Questions

1. Encryption is best defined as _____ .
   a. data that has not been tampered with intentionally or accidentally
   b. data that has been scrambled
   c. data that is secured so only intended users have access
   d. data that can be accessed when it is needed

2. In Windows Server 2003, who can access encrypted files? (Choose all that apply.)
   a. the owner of the files
   b. the administrator
   c. the recovery agent
   d. all users

3. If data that is encrypted with NTFS encryption is copied to a FAT partition, the data is decrypted. True or False?

4. What is the Windows Server 2003 command-line utility that can be used to encrypt data?
   a. Crypto
   b. EncryptIt
   c. Encrypt
   d. Cipher

5. You have decided to use NTFS encryption to enhance security on your network of six servers. Five of the six servers have compressed drives, and a new administrator says that it would not be a good idea to implement an encryption policy now. Why is or isn't the administrator correct?

   a. The administrator is not correct; encryption helps secure your network.

   b. The administrator is not correct; encryption decreases the performance of the servers, but is not noticeable to the users.

   c. The administrator is correct; encryption adds too much overhead to the servers.

   d. The administrator is correct; encryption and compression cannot be used at the same time.

8

CHAPTER NINE

USING AND MANAGING KEYS

Labs included in this chapter:

➤ Lab 9.1 Installing a Certificate Server

➤ Lab 9.2 Installing a Client Certificate

➤ Lab 9.3 Administering a Certificate Server

➤ Lab 9.4 Managing Personal Certificates

➤ Lab 9.5 Managing Certificate Revocation

CompTIA Security+ Exam Objectives	
Objective	Lab
Basics of Cryptography: PKI: Certificates	9.1, 9.2, 9.3, 9.4, 9.5

Lab 9.1 Installing a Certificate Server

Objectives

Servers running Certificate Services can perform as one of two types of certificate authorities (CAs): Enterprise or stand-alone. The Enterprise CA is part of Active Directory and has the ability to use templates and smart cards, and to publish certificates in Active Directory. The stand-alone CA does not require Active Directory and has no way to use templates. All certificates are marked pending until issued by an administrator. Certificates created on a stand-alone CA are not published and therefore must be distributed manually. In this lab, you will install Certificate Services and create a stand-alone root CA that is not a member of a Windows Server 2003 domain.

After completing this lab, you will be able to:

➤ Install Windows Server 2003 Certificate Services

➤ Configure a stand-alone root CA

Materials Required

This lab requires the following:

➤ A Windows Server 2003 server with Administrator access and an assigned ID number

➤ A Windows Server 2003 installation CD

> Estimated completion time: 20–25 minutes

Activity

1. Log on to your server as Administrator.

2. Click **Start**, and then click **Control Panel**.

3. Double-click **Add or Remove Programs**.

4. To install IIS, click **Add/Remove Windows Components**, highlight **Application Server**, and click **Details**.

5. Click the **Internet Information Services (IIS)** check box, and then click **OK**. IIS is required to manage certificates. Note that you might want to be more selective with IIS components you select outside this lab.

6. Click **Next**, and then click **Finish** when the installation is complete. You might be prompted for the Windows Server 2003 CD.

7. Click **Add/Remove Windows Components**.

8. Click the **Certificate Services** check box.

9. Click **Yes** to accept the warning message.

10. Click **Next**.

11. If necessary, select **Stand-alone root CA**, as shown in Figure 9-1.

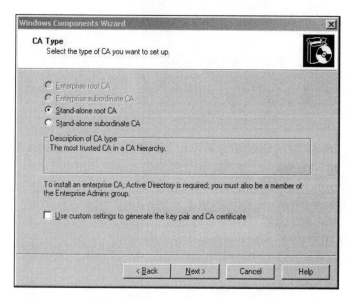

9

Figure 9-1   Selecting a stand-alone root CA

12. Click **Next**.

13. Enter the information shown in Figure 9-2. Replace X with your server number.

14. Click **Next**.

15. Click **Next** to accept the default Certificate database settings.

16. Click **Yes** to create the share and stop IIS.

17. You might be prompted for the Windows Server 2003 installation CD. If so, insert the CD and press **Enter**.

18. Click **Yes** to enable Active Server Pages.

19. Click **Finish**.

20. Close all windows and log off as Administrator. Remove the Windows Server 2003 CD, if necessary.

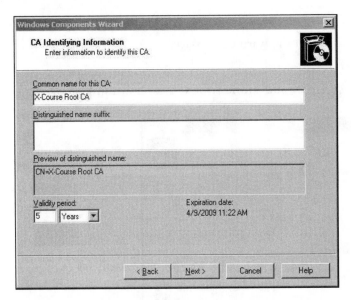

Figure 9-2   Entering CA identifying information

Certification Objectives

Objectives for CompTIA Security+ Exam:

➤ Basics of Cryptography: PKI: Certificates

Review Questions

1. Which of the following is best described as undeniable proof that a correspondence was sent or received?

    a. nonrepudiation

    b. return receipt

    c. mutual authentication

    d. verification

2. Which of the following uses a single key to encrypt and decrypt?

    a. public key

    b. symmetric key

    c. private key

    d. all of the above

3. Which of the following uses a pair of keys to encrypt and decrypt?

    a. public key

    b. symmetric key

    c. private key

    d. all of the above

4. Which of the following is a feature of a stand-alone CA?

    a. It is always trusted by all users and computers in its domain.

    b. It can use smart cards.

    c. It publishes certificates in Active Directory.

    d. none of the above

5. You can install a stand-alone CA on a server that participates in an Active Directory organization. True or False?

9

LAB 9.2 INSTALLING A CLIENT CERTIFICATE

Objectives

Windows Server 2003 servers that run Certificate Services and IIS have the ability to allow Web-based certificate requests. You can specify the type of certificate that you want and then wait for approval from an administrator. If you were using an Enterprise CA, the approval process would be automatic. Because you are using a stand-alone CA, however, the certificate is pending until approved. In this lab, you will create a certificate request, issue the certificate, and install it. All of these steps can be performed using a Web browser and the certificate authority MMC snap-in.

After completing this lab, you will be able to:

➤ Request a client certificate

➤ Install a client certificate

Materials Required

This lab requires the following:

➤ A Windows Server 2003 server with Administrator access

➤ The lab setup after completion of Lab 9.1

➤ A stand-alone CA

Estimated completion time: 20–25 minutes

LAB ACTIVITY

ACTIVITY

1. Log on to your server as Administrator.

2. Click **Start**, right-click **My Computer**, and select **Manage**.

3. Under System Tools, expand **Local Users and Groups**.

4. Right-click **Users** and select **New User**.

5. Enter the name **CertUserX** in the User name text box.

6. Uncheck the **User must change password at next logon** option.

7. Type **Pa$$word** in the Password and Confirm password text boxes.

8. Click **Create**, and then click **Close**.

9. Because you will log on to a stand-alone server, make the user a member of the **Power Users Group**.

10. Close all windows and log off.

11. Log on as **CertUserX** and start **Internet Explorer**.

12. Enter **http://server-x/certsrv** in the Address text box, and then press **Enter**. (Replace *server-x* with the name of your server.) You are warned that the site is blocked, as shown in Figure 9-3. Click **Add** twice to Trust the site, and then click **Close**. You should see a screen resembling the one shown in Figure 9-4.

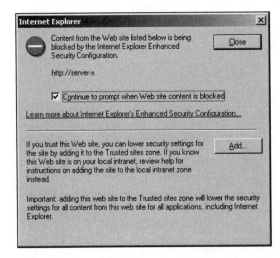

Figure 9-3   Notification that a Web site is blocked

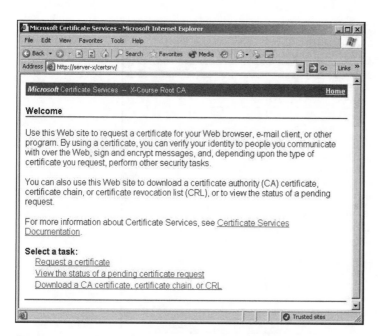

Figure 9-4   Microsoft Certificate Services window

13. Click **Request a certificate**.

14. Click **advanced certificate request**.

15. Click **Create and submit a request to this CA**.

16. Enter your identifying information using CertUserX as your name.

17. Accept the default values, as shown in Figure 9-5.

18. Click **Submit**, and then click **Yes** twice to request the certificate. When you see the certificate pending message, note your request ID number.

19. Close Internet Explorer and log off as CertUserX.

20. Log on as Administrator.

21. Click **Start**, click **Administrative Tools**, and then click **Certification Authority**.

22. Expand **X-Course Root CA** and select **Pending Requests**, as shown in Figure 9-6.

23. Right-click the **Certificate**, click **All Tasks**, and then click **Issue**. Click the **Issued Certificates** folder and notice that the certificate is there.

24. Log off as Administrator.

25. Log on to your server as CertUserX.

26. Start **Internet Explorer**.

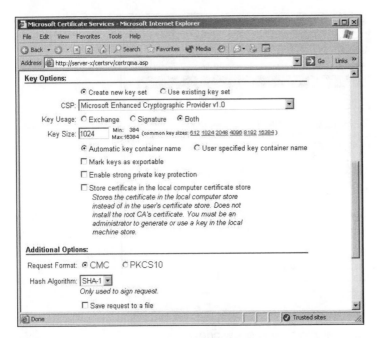

Figure 9-5   Accepting default Certificate Services settings

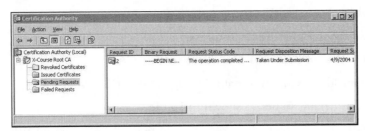

Figure 9-6   Issuing a certificate request

27. Enter **http://*server-x*/certsrv** in the Address text box, and then press **Enter**. (Replace *server-x* with the name of your server.)

28. Click **View the status of a pending certificate request**.

29. Click the link to your certificate.

30. Click **Install this certificate**. Click **Yes** to add the certificate. You should receive a message that the certificate was successfully installed.

31. Close all windows and log off.

Certification Objectives

Objectives for CompTIA Security+ Exam:

➤ Basics of Cryptography: PKI: Certificates

Review Questions

1. What is the maximum key length for Microsoft PKI components?

   a. 512 bits

   b. 1024 bits

   c. 2048 bits

   d. 4096 bits

2. What is the most common key length for PKI components?

   a. 512 bits

   b. 1024 bits

   c. 2048 bits

   d. 4096 bits

3. Which of the following is an example of a hash algorithm?

   a. MD4

   b. MD5

   c. SHA-1

   d. all of the above

4. By default, certificates are valid for _____ .

   a. one month

   b. one year

   c. two years

   d. two months

5. Certificates that have special characters in the organization name must be encoded in Unicode to remain compliant with the X.509 standard. True or False?

9

LAB 9.3 ADMINISTERING A CERTIFICATE SERVER

Objectives

Once you have the certificate authority up and running, you should be sure to perform preventive maintenance. You have the ability to stop and start the service without shutting down the server, which can help reduce downtime while troubleshooting a problem. You also can back up and restore the CA. This is a critical part of preventive maintenance, especially if you have a hardware failure and lose the CA. The CA can be backed up with Windows Server 2003 Backup or the integrated backup program that is part of the Certificate Services. These backups can be completed without stopping the service, but the restore requires you to restart the system. In this lab, you will stop and start the certificate authority and perform a backup and restore.

After completing this lab, you will be able to:

➤ Stop and start the certificate authority

➤ Back up and restore a certificate authority

Materials Required

This lab requires the following:

➤ A Windows Server 2003 server with Administrator access

➤ The lab setup after completion of Lab 9.2

➤ A stand-alone root CA

Estimated completion time: 20–25 minutes

LAB ACTIVITY

ACTIVITY

1. Log on as Administrator.

2. Click **Start**, click **Administrative Tools**, and then select **Certification Authority**.

3. Right-click the **X-Course Root CA**, click **All Tasks**, and then click **Stop Service**.

4. Once the service has stopped, repeat Step 3 and click **Start Service**.

5. Open My Computer and create a folder named **C:\CABackup**.

6. In the Certification Authority window, right-click the **X-Course Root CA**, click **All Tasks**, and then click **Back up CA**.

7. Click **Next** to begin the Certification Authority Backup Wizard.

8. Check the boxes for the items you want to back up and enter the backup path, as shown in Figure 9-7.

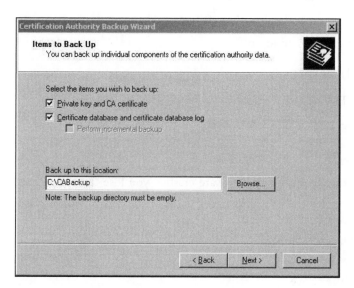

Figure 9-7   Selecting items to back up

9. Click **Next**.

10. Enter **password** in the Password and Confirm password text boxes.

11. Click **Next**.

12. Click **Finish**.

13. Using My Computer, confirm that the backup was successful by looking at the following files:
    - The **X-Course Root CA.p12** file in the CABackup folder
    - **certbkxp.dat**, **edb00001.log**, and **X-Course Root CA.edb** in the Database folder

14. In the Certification Authority window, right-click the **X-Course Root CA**, click **All Tasks**, and then click **Restore CA**.

15. Click **OK** to stop Certificate Services.

16. Click **Next**.

17. Check all boxes to restore everything.

18. Browse to the **C:\CABackup** folder.

19. Click **Next**.

20. Enter **password** in the Password text box and click **Next**.

21. Click **Finish**.

22. Click **Yes** to restart Certificate Services.

23. Restart the server to finalize the settings.

24. Close all windows and log off.

Certification Objectives

Objectives for CompTIA Security+ Exam:

➤   Basics of Cryptography: PKI: Certificates

Review Questions

1. If your certificate authority hardware crashes, you lose the ability to
_____ .

   a. issue certificates

   b. revoke certificates

   c. renew certificates

   d. all of the above

2. The certificate authority service must be stopped to perform a backup using the Certification Authority Backup Wizard. True or False?

3. Which of the following is only available to back up in a stand-alone CA environment?

   a. private key and CA certificate

   b. configuration information

   c. Issued Certificate Log and pending certificate request queue

   d. all of the above

4. Public key cryptography is also known as _____ .

   a. PGP

   b. 3DES

   c. Diffie-Hellman

   d. RSA

5. The Data Encryption Standard (DES) uses a _____ -bit key.

   a. 48

   b. 56

   c. 128

   d. 168

Lab 9.4 Managing Personal Certificates

Objectives

At some point you might need to import or export your certificates. For instance, you might want to export a certificate for a backup or for use on another computer, or you might want to import a certificate for a restore or import a certificate sent to you by another user or computer. The file format used by Windows Server 2003 is Personal Information Exchange (PKCS#12). This file type enables the transfer of certificates and their keys from one computer to another. In this lab, you will export and import a certificate.

After completing this lab, you will be able to:

➤ Export a certificate

➤ Import a certificate

Materials Required

This lab requires the following:

➤ A Windows Server 2003 server with Administrator access

➤ The lab setup after completion of Lab 9.3

➤ A stand-alone root CA

Estimated completion time:	20–25 minutes

LAB ACTIVITY

Activity

To prepare to export a certificate:

1. Log on to your server as Administrator.

2. Click **Start** and then click **Run**. Type **mmc** and press **Enter**.

3. Click **File** on the menu bar, and then click **Add/Remove Snap-in**.

4. Click **Add**, and then click **Certificates**.

5. Click **Add**, and then click **Finish**.

6. Click **Close**, and then click **OK**.

7. Expand **Certificates – Current User**.

8. Expand **Personal**, and then click **Certificates**, as shown in Figure 9-8.

9. View the certificate for CertUserX by double-clicking the name.

10. Click **OK** to close the window.

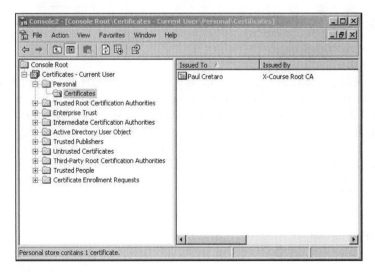

Figure 9-8 Preparing to export a certificate

To export a certificate:

1. Right-click the certificate.

2. Select **All Tasks**, and then click **Export**.

3. Click **Next** to begin the Certificate Export Wizard.

4. Click **Next** and accept the default options. *Note that the private key cannot be exported.*

5. Click **Next**.

6. Browse to **My Documents** and then enter **CertExport** for the name of the file.

7. Click **Save** and then click **Next**.

8. Click **Finish** and then click **OK**.

To import a certificate:

1. Start Windows Explorer.

2. Navigate to **My Documents**.

3. Right-click the **CertExport** certificate.

4. Click **Install Certificate**.

5. Click **Next** to begin the wizard.

6. Click **Next** to accept the default **Certificate Store**.

7. Click **Finish** and then click **OK**.

8. Close all windows and log off as Administrator.

Certification Objectives

Objectives for CompTIA Security+ Exam:

➤   Basics of Cryptography: PKI: Certificates

Review Questions

1. Which of the following is the most widely used standard for digital certificates?

    a. X.400

    b. X.500

    c. X.25

    d. X.509

2. You can safely distribute your public key to others. True or False?

3. A third-party certificate authority is always external to a company. True or False?

4. Which of the following certificate file formats are supported by Windows Server 2003? (Choose all that apply.)

    a. PKCS#12

    b. PKCS#7

    c. DER Encoded Binary X.500

    d. Base64 Encoded X.509

5. If people want to send you encrypted mail, they must have your _____ .

    a. private key

    b. public key

    c. S/MIME key

    d. all of the above

LAB 9.5 MANAGING CERTIFICATE REVOCATION

Objectives

Certificates are used to verify the identity of users on a network. However, certificates are not 100% effective and can be compromised at times. Therefore, you need the ability to revoke certificates. This is an easy process, in which you can also specify a reason for the revocation. In this lab, you will revoke a certificate and evaluate the results.

After completing this lab, you will be able to:

➤ Revoke a certificate

➤ View the certificate revocation list

Materials Required

This lab requires the following:

➤ A Windows Server 2003 server with Certificate Services installed

➤ The lab setup after completion of Lab 9.2

➤ Administrator access to the server

Estimated completion time: 15 minutes

ACTIVITY

1. Log on as Administrator.

2. Click **Start**, click **Administrative Tools**, and then click **Certification Authority**.

3. Expand **X-Course Root CA**.

4. Click **Issued Certificates**.

5. Right-click the **CertUserX** certificate, click **All Tasks**, and then click **Revoke Certificate**.

6. Select **Key Compromise** in the Reason code list box, as shown in Figure 9-9.

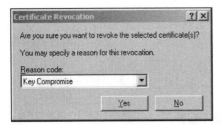

Figure 9-9 Managing certificate revocation

7. Click **Yes**.

8. Click **Revoked Certificates**. Notice the certificate.

9. Right-click **Revoked Certificates**, click **All Tasks**, and then click **Publish**.

10. Click **OK**.

11. Right-click **Revoked Certificates**, and then select **Properties**.

12. Click the **View CRLs** tab, and then click **View CRL**.

13. View the contents of the General and Revocation List tabs to verify that the certificate was revoked.

14. Close all windows and log off as Administrator.

Certification Objectives

Objectives for CompTIA Security+ Exam:

➤ Basics of Cryptography: PKI: Certificates

Review Questions

9

1. Which of the following is a reason to revoke a certificate?

   a. The key was lost.

   b. The key is known to someone else.

   c. The key has been compromised.

   d. all of the above

2. Once you revoke a certificate using Windows Server 2003 Certificate Services, it cannot be recovered. True or False?

3. In January 2001, _____ issued two fraudulent certificates to people claiming to be Microsoft.

   a. Verisign

   b. Sun

   c. Microsoft

   d. Entrust.net

4. Because of fraudulent certificates, it is safer to host an internal certificate authority than an external certificate authority. True or False?

5. Once you install Certificate Services, you cannot change the name of the computer if it is a stand-alone or Enterprise server. True or False?

OPERATIONAL SECURITY

Labs included in this chapter:

➤ Lab 10.1 Establishing Physical Barriers

➤ Lab 10.2 Using Biometrics

➤ Lab 10.3 Managing the Environment

➤ Lab 10.4 Understanding Social Engineering

CompTIA Security+ Exam Objectives	
Objective	Lab
Operational/Organizational Security: Physical Security: Access Control	10.1, 10.2
Operational/Organizational Security: Physical Security: Environment	10.3
Operational/Organizational Security: Physical Security: Social Engineering	10.4

Lab 10.1 Establishing Physical Barriers

Objectives

To maintain security in your building, its perimeter needs to be secured. Gating and lock systems are the primary methods for establishing a secure building. In an ideal world, a single point of entry would be used to "herd" all traffic into a facility. In most cases, however, buildings have multiple points of entry. Information security professionals must use the viewpoint of a burglar when surveying a site for physical vulnerabilities, starting with the perimeter. In the activity to follow, you have an opportunity to put this viewpoint to work, to see if you can identify perimeter vulnerabilities.

After completing this lab, you will be able to:

➤ Establish physical barriers to protect a facility

➤ Diagnose weaknesses in a facility's physical barrier protection

Materials Required

This lab requires the following:

➤ Paper and pen or pencil

➤ Visio or other flow-chart software (optional)

Estimated completion time: 45–60 minutes

Activity

Determining the perimeter strength of a site is also known as taking a site survey. This process requires an information security professional to physically examine a facility's various points of entry and determine their weaknesses and strengths.

For this lab activity, go to a local public facility of your choice and observe the physical barriers in place. Some examples of a public facility include a library, town hall, local grocery store, or local retail store. You can perform your site survey by walking or driving around the facility. When you finish your observations, draw a rough map of the grounds. Indicate the location of any fencing, gates, the main entrance, side entrances, and loading docks. When you return to the classroom, use your flow-chart software to prepare a report or diagram of the physical barriers.

Do not violate posted or nonposted trespassing rules of the facility. If you are not certain whether you are permitted in a particular location, do not go there.

NOTE

After completing this activity, share your results with the class for discussion:

1. Take turns drawing your surveillance maps on the white board, or distribute your drawings to your classmates.

2. What perimeter weaknesses did you observe?

3. What perimeter strengths did you observe?

4. What would you change? What would you not change?

5. Would you want to keep your personal information in this facility? Why or why not?

Certification Objectives

Objectives for CompTIA Security+ Exam:

➤ Operational/Organizational Security: Physical Security: Access Control

Review Questions

10

1. Which of the following is a preventive physical barrier?

   a. fences and gates

   b. selection of a nonshared facility

   c. security guard patrols

   d. all of the above

2. Which of the following is a reactive physical security control?

   a. biometric devices

   b. sign-in log

   c. mantrap entrances

   d. all of the above

3. Which of the following is the most expensive physical security control?

   a. procedural controls

   b. hardware devices

   c. electronic systems

   d. personnel

4. Which of the following measures provides a first line of defense against potential risks and threats to a computer center?

   a. application security

   b. data security

   c. physical security

   d. telecommunications security

5. What should be done first when a fire is detected in a facility?

    a. Activate the fire suppression system.

    b. Evacuate the building.

    c. Call the fire department.

    d. Use fire extinguishers to put out the fire.

LAB 10.2 USING BIOMETRICS

Objectives

Biometrics is a security control that identifies a person based on the examination of personal attributes, such as voiceprints or fingerprints. This type of high-tech authentication is often seen in movies, and is becoming more common in secure facilities. The secure storage of authentication data is the key to preventing inappropriate access. It is difficult to exploit biometric systems at the point of authentication, which is their main benefit.

After completing this lab, you will be able to:

➤ Understand appropriate uses for biometric technology

➤ Identify challenges associated with biometric technology

Materials Required

This lab requires the following:

➤ A computer with Internet access

Estimated completion time: 20 minutes

LAB ACTIVITY

ACTIVITY

Because biometrics is still an evolving technology, access to such devices is somewhat limited. However, manufacturers are competing to be leaders in the race to offer biometric authentication devices that are cost-effective and technologically superior. This activity requires Internet research to determine the current leaders in biometric devices. Your tasks are as follows:

1. Search the Internet to identify leading biometrics manufacturers.

2. Record the names of vendors that are currently leading the biometrics marketplace.

3. List any vulnerabilities associated with the biometrics devices you find.

Certification Objectives

Objectives for CompTIA Security+ Exam:

➤ Operational/Organizational Security: Physical Security: Access Control

Review Questions

1. Which of the following is an example of a biometric device?

   a. single-factor authentication

   b. multifactor authentication

   c. retinal scanner

   d. proximity badge

2. Which of the following authenticates a user's access based on a personal identification factor?

   a. biometrics

   b. access badge

   c. password

   d. lock

3. Biometrics is widely used to protect personal desktop computers. True or False?

4. Which of the following is the most reliable biometric authentication technique?

   a. password

   b. fingerprint

   c. voice verification

   d. iris scan

5. A retinal scan is a scan of the _____ .

   a. eye

   b. face

   c. voice

   d. palm

10

LAB 10.3 MANAGING THE ENVIRONMENT

Objectives

There are many components to managing a safe and secure environment. They range from fire protection and perimeter protection to humidity and temperature controls. Regardless of the environmental component being addressed by the security professional, the foremost concern is always the safety of personnel. This lab focuses on considerations for establishing escape routes and fire suppression. When managing control factors relating to fire suppression, security professionals should consider the following:

➤ *Potential fuel sources for fire*—Determine whether oxygen and combustible materials are kept in your facility.

➤ *Building contents*—Determine what dangerous or combustible materials are present in your facility, and the best way to extinguish them in case of fire.

➤ *Fire detection*—The more quickly a fire is detected, the greater your opportunity to safely evacuate the premises and minimize damage.

➤ *Fire extinguishing*—Fire suppression comes in many forms, including sprinkler systems, halon systems, fire extinguishers, and water. Determine which systems are best for your facility, depending on the materials stored there.

After completing this lab, you will be able to:

➤ Establish fire suppression controls to protect a facility

➤ Diagnose weaknesses in a facility's fire suppression protection

Materials Required

This lab requires the following:

➤ Paper and pen or pencil

➤ Flow-chart software (optional)

Estimated completion time: 45–60 minutes

ACTIVITY

This activity is another field trip. Take a walking tour of your school (or other public facility) with paper and pencil in hand. Your assignment is to draw a rough draft of the floor plan. On the floor plan, indicate the location of sprinkler heads, fire extinguishers, and fire alarm triggers. For each fire extinguisher, take note of the next and last inspection dates. Verify that the extinguishers are up to date with inspections. At the completion of this activity, share your results with the class for discussion.

1. Take turns drawing your floor plans on the white board.

2. What fire suppression controls did you observe?

3. Were the fire suppression controls adequate?

4. What would you change? What would you not change?

5. Would you feel safe in this facility?

Certification Objectives

Objectives for CompTIA Security+ Exam:

➤ Operational/Organizational Security: Physical Security: Environment

Review Questions

1. Electrical fires are classified as _____ .
   a. class A fires
   b. class B fires
   c. class C fires
   d. class D fires

2. Which of the following is an appropriate control in a computer room?
   a. smoke detection equipment that shuts down the wet-pipe equipment
   b. smoke detection equipment that shuts down the air-conditioning equipment
   c. smoke detection equipment that shuts down the UPS
   d. smoke detection equipment that shuts down the badge access controls

3. Where is the best place to sound an alarm from a computer center?
   a. receptionist desk
   b. guard station
   c. fire and police station
   d. CEO's office

4. What instrument is used to measure humidity levels in a computer center?
   a. hydrometer
   b. hygrometer
   c. barometer
   d. voltmeter

5. The most important asset to protect in a facility is the computer center. True or False?

LAB 10.4 UNDERSTANDING SOCIAL ENGINEERING

Objectives

Social engineering refers to the act of tricking people into divulging their password or information about network vulnerabilities. For example, a person might pretend to be someone else to gain some level of access that he should not have. Other components of social engineering include eavesdropping and snooping in places where you do not belong.

In general, people are the weakest link in the information security field. At some level we all have a desire to help others, and are often quick to provide answers to questions when we should be more wary. Another overlooked item is the privacy and protection of retired items, otherwise known as trash. That's right: one man's trash is a hacker's treasure. The following activity helps you hone your social engineering skills and then apply them to educate others in using common sense in this area.

After completing this lab, you will be able to:

➤ Improve your habits for protecting personal information

➤ Educate others on best practices for defending against social engineering attacks

Materials Required

This lab requires the following:

➤ Paper and pen or pencil

Estimated completion time: 45–60 minutes

ACTIVITY

1. Practice your active listening skills.

   Over a period of one week you can hear an amazing amount of information—if you listen. Your first task is to keep a diary of private information you hear from your friends, family, fellow students, and co-workers. For example, in an office environment with cubicles, co-workers often have conversations that are far too revealing. Maybe they are refinancing their home, so they give out their social security number, or perhaps you hear them give their account number to their bank over the phone.

NOTE

Do not invade anyone's privacy for this activity. Just listen closely, in public situations, to what other people say.

2. After compiling this list for a week, discreetly let people know what you heard them say, and gently caution them to be more careful with their public conversations.

3. At the end of this activity, share your results with the class for discussion, omitting the private information you have collected.

4. Another component of social engineering is snooping. For this activity, get ready to roll up your sleeves and get dirty—literally. It's time to do a little trash picking. Your assignment is to take one bag of your trash, empty it, and go through it, to see what a hacker might use to gain access to your private, electronic information. Examples of what you might find include bills with account numbers, bank statements, old checks, and important documents that display your social security number.

NOTE

You must pick through your own trash, not someone else's. Do not choose a trash can that other people use.

10

5. When you finish, discuss your findings with your classmates.

Certification Objectives

Objectives for CompTIA Security+ Exam:

➤ Operational/Organizational Security: Physical Security: Social Engineering

Review Questions

1. What kind of attack is used to persuade a user or administrator to give out information or access?

    a. DDoS attack

    b. social engineering attack

    c. SYN attack

    d. all of the above

2. Social engineering requires strong technical skills. True or False?

3. Who is susceptible to a social engineering attack?

    a. the CEO

    b. the system administrator

    c. the Help desk

    d. all of the above

4. Which is the best tactic to prevent social engineering?

   a. Implement training and awareness programs.

   b. Implement strong policies.

   c. Threaten to fire employees who give out information.

   d. Install surveillance systems.

5. How should you securely dispose of documents?

   a. Use a vertical shredder.

   b. Use a cross-shredder.

   c. Tear the document into pieces.

   d. Cross out private information and throw the document away.

CHAPTER ELEVEN

POLICIES AND PROCEDURES

Labs included in this chapter:

➤ Lab 11.1 Creating Security Policies (Remote Access)

➤ Lab 11.2 Creating Security Policies (Regulations)

➤ Lab 11.3 Performing Risk Analysis

CompTIA Security+ Exam Objectives	
Objective	Lab
Operational/Organizational Security: Policy and Procedures: Security Policy	11.1, 11.2
Operational/Organizational Security: Risk Identification	11.3

LAB 11.1 CREATING SECURITY POLICIES (REMOTE ACCESS)

Background

You have just been hired as a network security analyst for Acme Cleansers, a large company specializing in the manufacture of a unique cleaning product. The company has 10,000 employees worldwide and continues to grow every year. Management has decided to hire a security expert because a few recent security breaches have caused significant downtime for the company. The most recent event was a DDoS attack that prevented customers from making purchases for two full days. Over the past year the company has had over 10 days of downtime caused by similar attacks. Even though the company is very profitable, the downtime has resulted in many unhappy clients. Your job is to evaluate the situation and make recommendations to the IT management staff. You have decided to follow these steps:

➤ Document the current security configurations.

➤ Interview management and employees from each department.

➤ Recommend a security policy.

During the documentation phase you discovered the following:

➤ The company has a firewall, but it is not configured properly.

➤ The company has virus-scanning software on all of the desktop computers, and the signatures are managed by individual users.

➤ The company has a single Windows Server 2003 domain consisting of 11 sites with the following properties:

■ The file systems are a mix of FAT32 and NTFS.

■ All users are local administrators.

■ No Windows security policies exist—not even a password policy.

■ Auditing is not enabled.

■ Internet access is not monitored or filtered.

■ E-mail is not protected with virus protection software.

During the interview phase you discovered the following:

➤ Employees have not been trained on the basics of computer security.

➤ Most employees are using blank passwords.

➤ Employees say they spend an average of two hours per day surfing the Internet. (If they are willing to admit to two hours, it could actually be closer to four.)

➤ Most employees have lost data because of a virus outbreak.

➤ Employees have access to the company network via their personal ISP and a VPN connection. The VPN uses PPTP with PAP authentication.

During the recommendation phase you decided to do the following:

➤ Submit a document that summarizes your findings.

➤ Create a basic security policy template in specific areas so that the company can maintain and expand the policy in the future.

Objectives

Setting security policies is an important first step in securing data in your organization. These policies make it more difficult for hackers to infiltrate your defenses, and they promote good habits in users. In this lab you will create security policies that cover remote access to your network.

After completing this lab, you will be able to:

➤ Create an overall security policy

➤ Create a remote access policy

➤ Create a third-party network connection agreement

➤ Create an antivirus process

➤ Create a VPN security policy

Materials Required

This lab requires the following:

➤ A computer with Internet access

Estimated completion time: 90 minutes

LAB ACTIVITY

ACTIVITY

1. Visit the SANS Institute Web site and create a simple security policy for the company described earlier in this lab. The Web site is at *www.sans.org/resources/policies*.

2. Review the SANS security policy primer at *www.sans.org/resources/policies/#primer*.

3. Create a document for the board of directors that reports your findings about the current state of security at Acme Cleansers.

11

4. Create a security policy for the following areas using the templates at *www.sans.org/resources/policies/#template.*

   ■ A remote access policy
   ■ A third-party network connection agreement
   ■ An antivirus process
   ■ A VPN security policy

Certification Objectives

Objectives for CompTIA Security+ Exam:

➤ Operational/Organizational Security: Policy and Procedures: Security Policy

Review Questions

1. Which of the following defines and describes acceptable methods of connecting to an internal network from an outside source?

   a. remote access
   b. information protection
   c. perimeter security
   d. acceptable use
   e. none of the above

2. Which of the following defines and describes how physical security is maintained?

   a. remote access
   b. information protection
   c. perimeter security
   d. acceptable use
   e. none of the above

3. Arrange the following incident response categories in their proper order of completion in response to a virus incident.

   a. Identify the problem.
   b. Isolate the system.
   c. Notify the necessary people.

4. Which of the following is a level 1 security incident?

   a. sharing of user accounts
   b. computer virus infection
   c. employee termination
   d. abuse of access privileges

5. Which of the following is a level 3 security incident?

   a. sharing of user accounts

   b. computer virus infection

   c. employee termination

   d. abuse of access privileges

LAB 11.2 CREATING SECURITY POLICIES (REGULATIONS)

Objectives

Security policies are becoming more important because of recent government regulations such as the Sarbanes-Oxley Act on IT Security. The act requires companies to comply with regulations that are not yet completely clear, but companies have the advantage of being able to interpret the regulations in ways they think are sufficient. In the future, standards and best practices will be published. If companies prepare for these future regulations, the transition will be much easier when the standards and best practices are released.

After completing this lab, you will be able to:

➤ Create a security policy

➤ Create an acceptable-use policy

➤ Create a password protection policy

➤ Create an audit vulnerability scanning policy

➤ Create an e-mail retention policy

Materials Required

This lab requires the following:

➤ A computer with Internet access

Estimated completion time: 90 minutes

LAB ACTIVITY

ACTIVITY

1. Visit the SANS Institute Web site to continue developing the security policy for Acme Cleansers, the company described in Lab 11.1. The Web site is at *www.sans.org/resources/policies/policies.htm*.

2. Create a security policy for the following areas using the templates at *www.sans.org/resources/policies/#template.*
   - An acceptable-use policy
   - A password protection policy
   - An audit vulnerability scanning policy
   - An e-mail retention policy

Certification Objectives

Objectives for CompTIA Security+ Exam:

➤ Operational/Organizational Security: Policy and Procedures: Security Policy

Review Questions

1. Policies have the greatest effect on _____ .
   a. managers
   b. users
   c. IT staff
   d. auditors

2. Categorize each of the following as either "M" (what policies must do) or "S" (what policies should do).
   a. Describe what is covered by the policies.
   b. State why the policy is needed.
   c. Be implemented and enforceable.
   d. Define contacts and responsibilities.
   e. Be concise and easy to understand.
   f. Balance protection with productivity.
   g. Discuss how violations will be handled.

3. You must have management support to be able to implement a security policy. True or False?

4. Who should serve on a security committee to determine security policy requirements?
   a. management
   b. IT staff
   c. users
   d. all of the above

5. Which of the following are reasons for resistance to security policies? (Choose all that apply.)

   a. Employees do not like change.

   b. Security policies are illegal.

   c. Employees fear being spied on.

   d. all of the above

LAB 11.3 PERFORMING RISK ANALYSIS

Background

You are an IT manager for Acme Books, an e-commerce company that competes with *Amazon.com*. You are trying to justify the implementation of security and disaster recovery upgrades. The company has 5000 employees with three North American offices in New York, Los Angeles, and Montreal, and two offices overseas, in London and Paris. You recently experienced problems with the hardware and software used to run the e-commerce site. These problems resulted in 15 hours of downtime during prime business hours. Upper management sent you a message asking you to explain why the problems are occurring and encouraging you to prevent these events in the future. You feel that it is a good time to perform a risk analysis for the company. You have decided to follow these steps:

➤ Identify the knowledge level of all employees in the company.

➤ Determine security requirements.

➤ Identify vulnerabilities.

➤ Develop a protection plan.

During the knowledge phase you discovered the following:

➤ Upper management is aware of the cost of downtime.

➤ Upper management does not know why the downtime is occurring.

➤ Users are not aware of the cost associated with downtime.

➤ Users have been trained only on the sales software and Microsoft Office.

➤ No one outside the IT Department understands the complex design of the e-commerce system.

➤ Customers are beginning to complain about downtime.

During the security-requirement phase you discovered the following:

➤ A network diagram does not exist.

➤ Physical building security does not exist.

➤ Access to the network operations center is not controlled.

➤ The firewall service agreement was never used and has expired.

➤ The virus-scanning service agreement has also expired.

During the vulnerability phase you discovered the following:

➤ The firewall has not been updated for three years.

➤ Administrators use Telnet and FTP for remote access to the network servers.

➤ Users are local administrators of their PCs.

➤ Users have not been trained on the impact of computer viruses.

➤ Users have unknowingly installed spyware on their PCs.

➤ Some users have disabled their virus-scanning software.

➤ Servers are not clustered or load-balanced.

➤ The backup method is sufficient, but the tapes are located on site.

During the protection-plan phase you decided to do the following:

➤ Submit a document that summarizes your risk analysis.

➤ Submit a plan to upgrade the necessary areas of the IT infrastructure.

Objectives

A thorough analysis of the state of security on your network can help you identify weaknesses that might pose security risks. This analysis can serve many purposes. Identifying problem areas can show upper management that resources need to be devoted to the problem. This process can also help you focus your attention and resources in the most appropriate directions.

After completing this lab, you will be able to:

➤ Understand the complexity of risk analysis

➤ Create a risk analysis report using the OCTAVE method as a guide

Materials Required

This lab requires the following:

➤ A computer with Internet access

Estimated completion time:	90 minutes

LAB ACTIVITY

ACTIVITY

In this activity you will visit the CERT Web site and perform risk analysis for Acme Books, the company in the preceding scenario.

1. Review the introduction to the OCTAVE method at *www.cert.org/octave/ methodintro.html*.

2. Using the OCTAVE method, create a risk analysis report for the following areas:

- Phase 1: Build asset-based threat profiles
  - Process 1: Identify senior management knowledge
  - Process 2: Identify operational area knowledge
  - Process 3: Identify staff knowledge
  - Process 4: Create threat profiles
- Phase 2: Identify infrastructure vulnerabilities
  - Process 5: Identify key components
  - Process 6: Evaluate selected components
- Phase 3: Develop a security strategy and plans
  - Process 7: Conduct risk analysis
  - Process 8: Develop a protection strategy

11

Certification Objectives

Objectives for CompTIA Security+ Exam:

➤ Operational/Organizational Security: Risk Identification

Review Questions

1. Arrange the following in their proper order within the forensic process.

   a. analysis

   b. collection

   c. examination

   d. preparation

   e. documentation

2. In network forensics, it is essential to keep track of the chain of custody when handling evidence. True or False?

3. When responding to an incident, you should do which of the following?

    a. Examine log files.

    b. Look for sniffers.

    c. Look for remote control programs.

    d. Look for file sharing programs.

    e. all of the above

4. If you are under attack from a hacker, what should you do first?

    a. Observe the attacker.

    b. Chase the attacker away.

    c. Back up the system.

    d. Catch the attacker.

5. If you want to prosecute an attacker, you should contact legal counsel immediately. True or False?

6. What is the primary reason that most computer crimes go unpunished?

    a. lack of education

    b. privacy issues

    c. lack of resources

    d. none of the above

7. A(n) _____ attack occurs when an attacker impersonates another system by using its IP address.

    a. DDoS

    b. IP spoofing

    c. IP splicing

    d. IP tampering

8. A(n) _____ attack occurs when an attacker denies legitimate users access to a system.

    a. DDoS

    b. IP spoofing

    c. IP splicing

    d. IP tampering

9. A(n) _____ attack occurs when an attacker hijacks an active session.

   a. DDoS

   b. IP spoofing

   c. IP splicing

   d. IP tampering

10. Which of the following is the first step of risk management?

    a. monitoring

    b. evaluation of control

    c. management

    d. threat assessment

    e. inventory

11. In which of the following stages of risk management is a vulnerability list created?

    a. monitoring

    b. evaluation of control

    c. management

    d. threat assessment

    e. inventory

12. Which of the following stages of risk management is ongoing as the process evolves?

    a. monitoring

    b. evaluation of control

    c. management

    d. threat assessment

    e. inventory

13. In what area of security management do you use an intrusion detection system (IDS)?

    a. Security Technology Management

    b. Vulnerability Management

    c. Systems Availability

11

14. In what area of security management do you maintain a library of attack signatures?

    a. Security Technology Management

    b. Vulnerability Management

    c. Exploitation Management

    d. Systems Availability

15. Who is typically responsible for overseeing the risk management process?

    a. IT manager

    b. chief executive officer

    c. chief financial officer

    d. chief security officer

SECURITY MANAGEMENT

Labs included in this chapter:

➤ Lab 12.1 Online Research—Awareness

➤ Lab 12.2 Online Research—Education

➤ Lab 12.3 Online Research—Standards and Guidelines

➤ Lab 12.4 Online Research—Classification

➤ Lab 12.5 Online Research—Retention and Storage

CompTIA Security+ Exam Objectives	
Objective	Lab
Security Management: Education: Online Resources	12.1, 12.2, 12.3, 12.4, 12.5
Security Management: Education: User Awareness	12.1
Security Management: Education	12.2
Security Management: Documentation: Standards and Guidelines	12.3
Security Management: Documentation: Classification	12.4
Security Management: Documentation: Retention/Storage	12.5

LAB 12.1 ONLINE RESEARCH—AWARENESS

Objectives

Securing a company or campus network extends well beyond technical preparation and application. Ensuring that the user community is aware of the security impacts is just as important. If users are not made aware of the ways they can affect security, they might unknowingly do something to damage the network. Before you prepare users to understand security, it is important to set guidelines for the training.

After completing this lab, you will be able to:

➤ Understand the importance of user awareness

➤ Create a document to outline a plan to make users more aware of security

➤ Create a distribution e-mail to notify the user community of future training

Materials Required

This lab requires the following:

➤ A Windows Server 2003 server with Internet access

Estimated completion time: 30–40 minutes

ACTIVITY

In this activity you will search the Internet for security documentation that covers user awareness.

   1. Start Internet Explorer and go to *www.sans.org/rr/*. Click the **Security Awareness** link, and then click the link called **Security Awareness: Help the Users Understand**.

You must scroll down the Web page to access some of the links mentioned in this chapter.

NOTE

   2. After reading the material, write a one- to two-page outline for security awareness guidelines.

   3. Using the outline, write a summary e-mail that can be sent to all employees, notifying them how security training will be given.

Certification Objectives

Objectives for CompTIA Security+ Exam:

➤ Security Management: Education: User Awareness

➤ Security Management: Education: Online Resources

Review Questions

1. What are the primary topics covered in security awareness programs?

    a. social engineering

    b. passwords

    c. viruses

    d. hoaxes

    e. all of the above

2. Which of the following security problems is the most difficult to track or discover?

    a. social engineering

    b. passwords

    c. viruses

    d. hoaxes

3. All passwords are capable of being cracked. True or False?

4. For which of the following is a policy easiest to enforce?

    a. social engineering

    b. passwords

    c. viruses

    d. hoaxes

5. The purpose of a security awareness program is to make sure that users understand their impact on the organization's resources. True or False?

12

LAB 12.2 ONLINE RESEARCH—EDUCATION

Objectives

Social engineering is the most common method used to gain unauthorized access to an organization's network. The process takes advantage of human nature. We tend to trust others and believe them, especially people in positions of authority. The first step in educating users is to make them aware of social engineering and its common methods.

After completing this lab, you will be able to:

➤ Understand the importance of preventing social engineering

➤ Create a lesson plan to help train users to avoid social engineering tactics

Materials Required

This lab requires the following:

➤ A Windows Server 2003 server with Internet access

Estimated completion time: 30–40 minutes

ACTIVITY

In this activity you will search the Internet for security documentation that educates users about social engineering.

1. Start Internet Explorer and go to ***www.sans.org/rr/***. Click the **Social Engineering** link, and then click the link called **A Proactive Defence to Social Engineering**.

2. After reading the material, write a lesson plan for a one-hour presentation to the user community regarding social engineering.

Certification Objectives

Objectives for CompTIA Security+ Exam:

➤ Security Management: Education

➤ Security Management: Education: Online Resources

Review Questions

1. Which of the following are methods used in social engineering? (Choose all that apply.)

   a. flattery

   b. sniffing

   c. name dropping

   d. imaging

2. What is the first thing a social engineer does when planning an attack?

   a. contacts the help desk immediately

   b. performs background research on the company

   c. applies for a job at the company

   d. none of the above

3. Which of the following roles would most likely produce the best results in a social engineering attack?

   a. impersonating an IT staff member

   b. impersonating a third-party vendor

   c. impersonating a manager

   d. impersonating a repairman

   e. impersonating an executive

4. A security awareness program should not only state the policies, it should educate users. True or False?

5. Help desks are vulnerable because they are the first line of support. True or False?

12

LAB 12.3 ONLINE RESEARCH—STANDARDS AND GUIDELINES

Objectives

In most organizations, security standards are practically nonexistent. Often, the more security you have, the less usability you have, so most organizations choose usability over security. But with the Internet's growth in popularity, security is becoming more important than ever. The Internet can open holes in an otherwise secure company, but companies also have the opportunity to set standards in the best way possible. Plenty of Internet sites contain standards and guidelines regarding information security.

After completing this lab, you will be able to:

➤ Understand the importance of standards and guidelines

➤ Create a document to outline a plan to implement security standards

Materials Required

This lab requires the following:

➤ A Windows Server 2003 server with Internet access

Estimated completion time: 30–40 minutes

LAB ACTIVITY

ACTIVITY

In this activity you will search the Internet for security documentation that covers security standards and guidelines.

1. Start Internet Explorer and go to *www.sans.org/rr/*. Click the **Standards** link. Next, click the link called **Organizational Information Security from Scratch – A Guarantee for Doing It Right**.

2. After reading the material, write a one- to two-page outline for security standards.

Certification Objectives

Objectives for CompTIA Security+ Exam:

➤ Security Management: Documentation: Standards and Guidelines

➤ Security Management: Education: Online Resources

Review Questions

1. The first step in developing security guidelines is _____ .
   a. risk assessment
   b. prevention
   c. software inventory
   d. creating roles
   e. documentation

2. Which of the following should be a part of determining security guidelines?
   a. help desk
   b. upper management
   c. CEO
   d. all of the above

3. It is important to have internal audits that evaluate security guidelines before they are fully implemented. True or False?

4. It is important that a security policy avoids conflicts with_____ .

   a. user opinions

   b. laws

   c. management opinions

   d. existing configurations

5. The growth of the Internet has decreased the need for a comprehensive security policy. True or False?

LAB 12.4 ONLINE RESEARCH—CLASSIFICATION

Objectives

In addition to the growth of the Internet, as mentioned in Lab 12.3, another facet of security management is new government regulations, which are forcing most organizations to comply with strict guidelines. Whether it is HIPAA for the medical field or Sarbanes-Oxley for the financial field, companies must comply with the new regulations. Failure to do so could cause organizations to be fined or even fail. The first step in developing guidelines is to classify the data.

After completing this lab, you will be able to:

➤ Understand the importance of information classification

➤ Create a one- to two-page document of information classification findings

Materials Required

This lab requires the following:

➤ A Windows Server 2003 server with Internet access

Estimated completion time: 30–40 minutes

ACTIVITY

In this activity you will search the Internet for security documentation that covers information classification.

1. Start Internet Explorer and go to **www.sans.org/rr/**. Click the **Auditing & Assessment** link. Next, click the link called **Information Classification – Who, Why and How**.

2. After reading the material, write a one- to two-page outline for information classification.

Certification Objectives

Objectives for CompTIA Security+ Exam:

➤ Security Management: Documentation: Classification

➤ Security Management: Education: Online Resources

Review Questions

1. Which of the following is crucial to information security?

   a. confidentiality

   b. integrity

   c. availability

   d. all of the above

   e. none of the above

2. An access method that is based on business need or job function is also known as _____ .

   a. administrative

   b. public

   c. role-based

   d. discretionary

3. The first step in classification is _____ .

   a. identifying sources that need to be protected

   b. identifying information classes

   c. identifying information protection measures

   d. identifying the appropriate use guidelines

4. Which of the following is used to ensure the integrity of information?

   a. technology control

   b. encryption

   c. administrative controls

   d. access control lists

5. Data classification ensures that the needs of the company as a whole are satisfied, instead of individual needs. True or False?

LAB 12.5 ONLINE RESEARCH—RETENTION AND STORAGE

Objectives

Data retention and storage are an important part of any organization. Data loss can have a direct impact on several areas of a business. It is important to set a policy for how long data will be available in the event of an outage or disaster. It isn't practical to keep everything forever, but a reasonable policy is needed. The policy that you set might depend on the needs of the organization as well as government regulations. Most importantly, the data needs to be available.

After completing this lab, you will be able to:

➤ Understand the importance of retention and storage

➤ Create a one- to two-page document on data retention

Materials Required

This lab requires the following:

➤ A Windows Server 2003 server with Internet access

12

Estimated completion time: 30–40 minutes

ACTIVITY

In this activity you will search the Internet for security documentation that covers data retention and storage.

1. Start Internet Explorer and go to **www.sans.org/rr/**. Click the **Backup Strategies** link, and then click the **Electronic Data Retention Policy** link.

2. After reading the material, write a one- to two-page outline of a data retention policy.

Certification Objectives

Objectives for CompTIA Security+ Exam:

➤ Security Management: Documentation: Retention/Storage

➤ Security Management: Education: Online Resources

Review Questions

1. Data needs to be retained for which of the following reasons?

   a. legal requirements

   b. personal requirements

   c. business requirements

   d. all of the above

   e. none of the above

2. The key behind data retention is to find the appropriate balance between too long (indefinite retention) and not long enough (premature destruction). True or False?

3. Which of the following should be documented first?

   a. legal requirements

   b. personal requirements

   c. business requirements

   d. none of the above

4. Which of the following is the least important for data retention and storage?

   a. legal requirements

   b. personal requirements

   c. business requirements

   d. none of the above

5. The law is years behind the technology, so the rules for data retention and storage are still being established. True or False?

CHAPTER THIRTEEN

ADVANCED SECURITY AND BEYOND

Labs included in this chapter:

➤ Lab 13.1 Transferring NTFS Encrypted Files

➤ Lab 13.2 Installing ZDelete and Restorer2000

➤ Lab 13.3 Using ZDelete Disk Wiper and Restorer2000

➤ Lab 13.4 Installing Microsoft Network Monitor

➤ Lab 13.5 Using Microsoft Network Monitor to Sniff an FTP Session

CompTIA Security+ Exam Objectives	
Objective	Lab
Infrastructure Security: Media	13.1, 13.2, 13.3, 13.4, 13.5

Lab 13.1 Transferring NTFS Encrypted Files

Objectives

An advanced feature of NTFS is the ability to encrypt files and folders. Unlike most encryption programs, NTFS encryption is transparent to the user. This is especially convenient for users who do not want to learn the details of the operating system, but who want to create data, encrypt it, and move on. However, transparent encryption does have a disadvantage: users need not know which data is encrypted, but they also are not notified about which data is decrypted, which opens a potential security hole.

After completing this lab, you will be able to:

➤ Encrypt a file on an NTFS partition

➤ Remove the encryption by copying the file to a floppy disk

Materials Required

This lab requires the following:

➤ A Windows Server 2003 server with an NTFS partition and Administrator access

➤ A 3½-inch floppy disk

```
Estimated completion time: 15 minutes
```

LAB ACTIVITY

Activity

1. Log on to your server as Administrator.

2. Click **Start**, right-click **My Computer**, and select **Explore**.

3. Navigate to **C:\Documents and Settings\Administrator**.

4. Right-click the **Start Menu** folder and select **Properties**.

5. Click the **Advanced** button.

6. Check the **Encrypt contents to secure data** option, as shown in Figure 13-1.

7. Click **OK**.

8. Click **OK**. You are asked to confirm your changes.

9. If necessary, click the **Apply changes to this folder, subfolders and files** option, as shown in Figure 13-2.

10. Click **OK**. Notice that the Start Menu folder is now green.

Figure 13-1   Encrypting contents

Figure 13-2   Confirming attribute changes

13

11. Insert the 3½-inch floppy disk in the disk drive. Right-click the **Start Menu** folder and select **Send To, 3½ Floppy (A:)**. Click **Ignore All** when prompted about encryption loss.

12. After the files are copied, navigate to the floppy-disk drive in My Computer and click its icon.

13. Right-click the **Start Menu** folder and select **Properties**. You see a window resembling the one shown in Figure 13-3. Notice that the Advanced button is no longer available. The files have been decrypted.

14. Close all open windows.

Certification Objectives

Objectives for CompTIA Security+ Exam:

➤ Infrastructure Security: Media

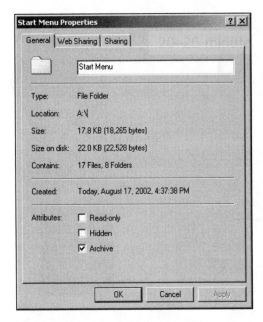

Figure 13-3   Start Menu properties

Review Questions

1. Which version of Windows supports NTFS encryption?

   a. Windows Server 2003

   b. Windows XP

   c. Windows NT 4 SP4

   d. all of the above

2. A file retains its encryption status if _____ .

   a. it is copied to a floppy disk

   b. it is compressed and then copied to a floppy disk

   c. it is copied to an NTFS partition

   d. it is copied to a FAT partition

3. Which of the following accounts can recover encrypted files?

   a. the owner's account

   b. the Administrator account

   c. the recovery agent account

   d. all of the above

4. If a disgruntled user deletes his keys before leaving a job, the administrator can log on as the user to decrypt the files. True or False?

5. If you attempt to encrypt a compressed folder, what happens?

    a. The compression remains.

    b. The compression is removed.

    c. The encryption is denied.

    d. The process is denied.

LAB 13.2 INSTALLING ZDELETE AND RESTORER2000

Objectives

When a file is deleted in Windows Server 2003, the operating system places the file in the Recycle Bin. This essentially removes the file from the directory listing, but space on the disk is still reserved. After the Recycle Bin is emptied, the file is removed from the file allocation table (FAT partitions) or master file table (MFT; NTFS partitions) and the first character is deleted. However, the file still exists on the hard drive until the space is overwritten by another file or by the defragmentation process. Recently deleted files can easily be recovered with the appropriate tools, such as Norton Utilities. Programs such as ZDelete were created to protect the privacy of confidential data. ZDelete can permanently erase data using a process that overwrites deleted files with random 1s and 0s, making the files impossible to recover. Otherwise, programs such as Restorer2000 can be used to restore deleted files.

13

After completing this lab, you will be able to:

➤ Install and configure the LSoft Technologies ZDelete program

➤ Install the Bitmart Inc. Restorer2000 program

Materials Required

This lab requires the following:

➤ A Windows Server 2003 server with Administrator access

➤ The LSoft Technologies ZDelete program, available at *www.zdelete.com*

➤ The Bitmart Inc. Restorer2000 program, available at *www.bitmart.net*

Estimated completion time: 20 minutes

LAB ACTIVITY

ACTIVITY

1. Download a free version of ZDelete. If you receive a message that the site is blocked, add the site by clicking the **Add** button, click **Add** again, and then click **Close**.

2. Open the **ZDeleteSetup.exe** setup file. Click **Next**.

3. Select the **I Agree to the terms of the license** option, and click **Next**.

4. Click **Next** to accept the default installation location, as shown in Figure 13-4. (Note that the intallation program might have changed slightly since this book's publication.)

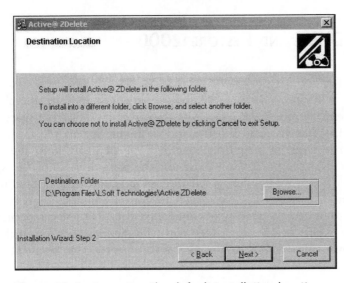

Figure 13-4   Accepting the default installation location

5. Select the **Program Files** and **Help** components to install, as shown in Figure 13-5. Click **Next**.

6. Click **Next** to start the installation.

7. After the files are copied, verify that the **Run ZDelete Wizard to configure software** option is checked and click **Finish**. The configuration wizard starts.

8. Click **Next**.

9. Accept the default settings in Step 2 of the wizard and click **Next**.

10. Click **Next** in Step 3 of the wizard without selecting any Custom Items.

11. Click **Next** to skip Step 4 of the wizard.

12. Click **Finish** to accept all default options, as shown in Figure 13-6.

13. Download a free version of Restorer2000. To start installing Restorer2000, double-click **r2k_demo.exe**.

14. Check the **I agree with the above terms and conditions** option and click **Next**.

15. Click **Start** to accept the default installation location.

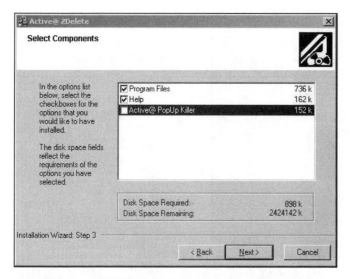

Figure 13-5   Selecting ZDelete components to install

13

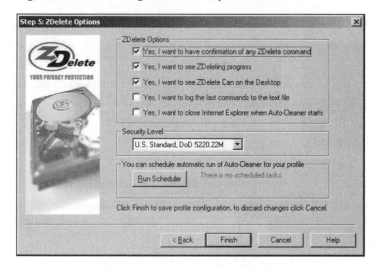

Figure 13-6   Accepting ZDelete default options

16. Uncheck the **Run Installed Application** option, as shown in Figure 13-7.

17. Click **OK**.

18. Close all windows and log off.

Certification Objectives

Objectives for CompTIA Security+ Exam:

➤ Infrastructure Security: Media

Figure 13-7 Installing Restorer2000

Review Questions

1. The NTFS MFT is created when an NTFS volume is formatted. True or False?

2. Which of the following commands can you enter to determine the size of the MFT in Windows NT?

    a. dir $mft

    b. dir /a $mft

    c. dir /s $mft

    d. none of the above; use a disk defragmenter instead

3. Which of the following commands can you enter to determine the size of the MFT in Windows Server 2003?

    a. dir $mft

    b. dir /a $mft

    c. dir /s $mft

    d. none of the above; use a disk defragmenter instead

4. When you empty the Recycle Bin, you cannot recover the files without a special utility. True or False?

5. If you want to delete a file without sending it to the Recycle Bin, you must hold down the _____ key while deleting.

 a. Shift

 b. Ctrl

 c. Alt

 d. F10

LAB 13.3 USING ZDELETE DISK WIPER AND RESTORER2000

Objectives

Occasionally, sensitive information in an organization needs to be stored somewhere other than the network, to prevent unauthorized access. In these cases, external media are used to store the information. The most common media used in these situations are floppy disks for small files and CDs or Zip disks for larger files. Sometimes, a disk or floppy disk must be wiped clean. Although you might want to destroy the disk, a more economical method is to use disk-cleaning software such as ZDelete Disk Wiper. After files have been wiped clean with Disk Wiper, programs such as Restorer2000 cannot recover the files.

After completing this lab, you will be able to:

➤ Use Restorer2000 to recover deleted files

➤ Use ZDelete Disk Wiper to completely erase files

Materials Required

This lab requires the following:

➤ A Windows Server 2003 server with Administrator access

➤ ZDelete Disk Wiper

➤ Restorer2000

13

Estimated completion time: 15 minutes

LAB ACTIVITY

ACTIVITY

1. Log on as Administrator.

2. Click **Start**, right-click **My Computer**, and select **Explore**.

3. Create three folders named **Recoverable**, **Unrecoverable**, and **Restore** on the root directory of your hard drive (C:).

4. In the **Recoverable** folder, create a text file named *YourName***Recoverable.txt** (replacing *YourName* with your name). In the file, type "This file will be recoverable." Save and close the file.

5. In the **Unrecoverable** folder, create a text file named *YourName***Unrecoverable.txt** (replacing *YourName* with your name). In the file, type "This file will be unrecoverable." Save and close the file.

6. Delete the file in the **Recoverable** folder.

7. Empty the Recycle Bin.

8. Click **Start**, click **All Programs**, click **Restorer2000 Demo**, and then click **Restorer2000 Demo**. You see a window resembling the one shown in Figure 13-8.

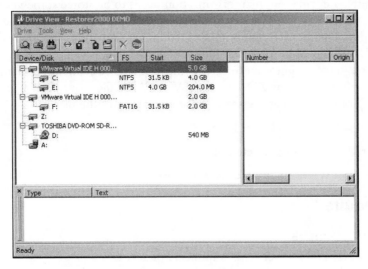

Figure 13-8 Starting the Restorer2000 demo

9. Right-click **C:** and select **Open Drive Files**.

10. Expand **Root** if necessary and navigate to the **RECYCLER** folder. This folder is created automatically.

11. Expand the folders until you find the text file you deleted in Step 6. Make a note of the new folder name. It should be Dc1, as the names are listed in numerical order. This name might vary, depending on what you have already deleted.

12. Right-click the folder that contains your text file, and select **Recover**.

13. Enter **c:\restore** in the **Output folder** text box, as shown in Figure 13-9.

14. Uncheck the **Ignore File Mask** option, if necessary, and then click **OK**. You receive the warning shown in Figure 13-10.

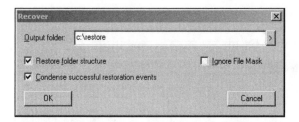

Figure 13-9   Specifying an output folder in Restorer2000

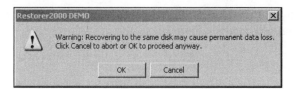

Figure 13-10   Restorer2000 warning

15. Click **OK**.

16. After the recovery is complete, close Restorer2000 and navigate to the **Restore** folder to find your file.

17. Navigate to the **Unrecoverable** folder and delete it.

18. Empty the Recycle Bin.

19. Click **Start**, click **My Computer**, and navigate to the **C:\RECYCLER** folder. (This is a protected system folder; to view it, you might have to click **Tools** on the menu bar of My Computer, click **Folder Options**, click the **View** tab, scroll down, remove the check next to **Hide protected operating system files**, click **Yes**, and click **OK**.)

20. Right-click the **RECYCLER** folder and select **ZDelete**.

21. Make sure that **C:\RECYCLER** is the only box checked. Click **Yes**.

22. When the program finishes, close all windows.

23. Click **Start**, click **All Programs**, click **Restorer2000 Demo**, and then click **Restorer2000 Demo**.

24. Right-click **C:** and select **Open Drive Files**.

25. Expand **Root** and navigate to the **RECYCLER** folder. Notice that the **Dc***x* file is not recoverable.

26. Close all windows and log off.

13

Certification Objectives

Objectives for CompTIA Security+ Exam:

➤   Infrastructure Security: Media

Review Questions

1. When you delete a file, the system simply replaces the first bit of the file with another bit. True or False?

2. Most files do not fully use the clusters allocated to them. This leftover space that might still contain old data is known as _____ .

    a. free space

    b. MFT space

    c. slack space

    d. leftover space

3. A file wiper overwrites unallocated areas with random data to prevent recovery. True or False?

4. Which of the following methods is the only true way to guarantee that data has been deleted?

    a. Empty the Recycle Bin.

    b. Destroy the hardware and all backups.

    c. FDISK the hard drive.

    d. Format the hard drive and then burn it.

5. Which of the following allow you to recover data after a disk has been wiped? (Choose all that apply.)

    a. CD-ROM archives

    b. backup tapes

    c. e-mail

    d. none of the above

Lab 13.4 Installing Microsoft Network Monitor

Objectives

Network Monitor is provided with Windows Server 2003 and offers basic network-sniffing features. It is a good learning tool, but it is limited to sniffing packets from the local network interface card (NIC). Microsoft also offers an enhanced version of Network Monitor that can operate in promiscuous mode and sniff packets from any computer on the network. You should use this product on a production network; it is packaged with Microsoft Systems Management Server.

After completing this lab, you will be able to:

➤ Install Network Monitor

➤ Configure Network Monitor to operate on the appropriate NIC

Materials Required

This lab requires the following:

➤ A Windows Server 2003 server with Administrator access

➤ A Windows Server 2003 installation CD

➤ Access to the NIC on your classroom network

| Estimated completion time: 15 minutes |

LAB ACTIVITY

ACTIVITY

1. Log on as Administrator.

2. Click **Start**, click **Control Panel**, and then double-click **Add or Remove Programs**.

3. Click **Add/Remove Windows Components**.

4. Highlight **Management and Monitoring Tools**, and then click **Details**.

5. Check the **Network Monitor Tools** option, and click **OK**.

6. Click **Next**. If prompted, insert the Windows Server 2003 CD, and then click **OK**.

7. Click **Finish**, and then click the **Close button** to close the Add or Remove Programs window.

8. Close the Control Panel.

9. Click **Start**, click **Run**, and type **cmd**. Press **Enter**.

10. At the command line, type **ipconfig /all**, press **Enter**, and write down the MAC address (also known as the Physical Address) of your network card.

11. Click **Start**, click **All Programs**, click **Administrative Tools**, and then select **Network Monitor**. You receive the message shown in Figure 13-11.

12. Click **OK**.

13

Figure 13-11   Prompt for specifying data-capture network

13. Expand **Local Computer** and select the appropriate NIC in the Properties list (the MAC address you wrote down in Step 10). The window resembles the one shown in Figure 13-12. Click **OK**.

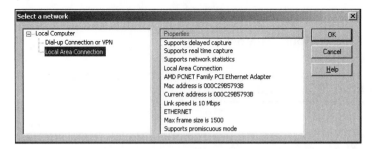

Figure 13-12   Choosing the NIC with the correct MAC address

14. Close all windows and log off.

Certification Objectives

Objectives for CompTIA Security+ Exam:

➤ Infrastructure Security: Media

Review Questions

1. By default, Network Monitor captures all data sent to your NIC. What can you use to narrow the scope of the data collected?

   a. a NIC in promiscuous mode

   b. a screen

   c. a filter

   d. a strainer

2. Network Monitor is considered a sniffer. Which of the following is a characteristic of a sniffer?

   a. logging

   b. fault analysis

      c. performance analysis

      d. all of the above

  3. Which layer 2 device can limit the functionality of sniffing?

      a. a bridge

      b. a hub

      c. a switch

      d. a brouter

  4. A packet is found at which layer of the OSI model?

      a. Physical

      b. Data Link MAC

      c. Data Link LLC

      d. Network

  5. A sniffer can be dangerous because it is very difficult to detect and can be attached to almost any part of a network. True or False?

LAB 13.5 USING MICROSOFT NETWORK MONITOR TO SNIFF AN FTP SESSION

13

Objectives

Although Network Monitor is a very useful networking utility, it can also be used maliciously. FTP and Telnet send usernames and passwords in clear text; Network Monitor can capture the entire FTP session and present the username and password to a potential hacker. One way to prevent this problem is to use only anonymous access for FTP sites. Unfortunately, this does not enable you to lock down access to the server. You can also configure the FTP server to only allow certain IP addresses, or use a VPN connection to limit access to the appropriate users.

After completing this lab, you will be able to:

➤ Capture an FTP session using Network Monitor

➤ Interpret the captured data to determine the username and password used

Materials Required

This lab requires the following:

➤ Two Windows Server 2003 servers with the FTP server and Network Monitor installed

➤ Administrator access to the servers

Estimated completion time: 15 minutes

ACTIVITY

1. On Server-X, log on as Administrator.

2. Click **Start**, right-click **My Computer**, and select **Manage**.

3. Expand **Services and Applications**.

4. Expand **Internet Information Services (IIS) Manager**, and then click **FTP Sites**. Make sure the **Default FTP Site** is started. Note that you installed the FTP service in Chapter 9.

5. Click **Start**, click **All Programs**, click **Administrative Tools**, and then select **Network Monitor**.

6. Click **Capture** on the menu bar, and then click **Start**.

7. On Server-Y, log on as Administrator.

8. Click **Start**, click **Run**, and then type **cmd**. Press **Enter**.

9. Type **ftp server-x** and then press **Enter**. Note that you can also use the IP address of Server-X.

10. Enter **Administrator** for the user, and then press **Enter**.

11. Enter **Pa$$word** (or your password) for the password, and then press **Enter**.

12. After you are logged on, type **quit** and then press **Enter**.

13. On Server-X, click **Capture** on the menu bar of Network Monitor, and then click **Stop and View**.

14. Examine Frames 10 and 13 in Figure 13-13. The user account and password are listed. Note that the frame numbers might be different on your capture, but the frames containing the user account and password are present.

15. Close all windows and log off Server-X and Server-Y.

Certification Objectives

Objectives for CompTIA Security+ Exam:

➤ Infrastructure Security: Media

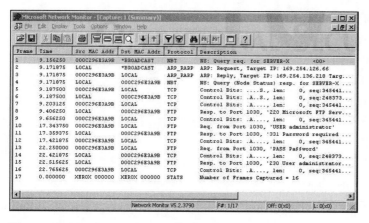

Figure 13-13   Using Microsoft Network Monitor

Review Questions

1. Network Monitor captures and displays which of the following?

    a. the source address

    b. the destination address

    c. protocols

    d. data

    e. all of the above

2. Which of the following security features is available with the full version of Network Monitor?

    a. Identify Network Monitor users

    b. Intrusion detection system add-on

    c. Packet modification tools

    d. Password sniffing tools

3. Network Monitor allows you to view encrypted data in plain text. True or False?

13

4. Which of the following protocols sends passwords and data in clear text?

   a. Telnet

   b. FTP

   c. HTTP

   d. NNTP

   e. IMAP

   f. POP

   g. SNMP

   h. all of the above

5. Which of the following protocols can be used to encrypt e-mail? (Choose all that apply.)

   a. PCP

   b. PGP

   c. MIME

   d. S/MIME